John Deere Tractors Worldwide
A Century of Progress
1893-1993

Don Macmillan

Published by the
American Society of Agricultural Engineers
2950 Niles Road, St. Joseph, Michigan

About ASAE — The Society for engineering in agricultural, food, and biological systems

ASAE is a technical and professional organization of members committed to improving agriculture through engineering. Many of our 10,000 members in the United States, Canada, and more than 100 other countries are engineering professionals actively involved in designing the farm equipment that continues to help the world's farmers feed the growing population. We're proud of the triumphs of the agriculture and equipment industry. ASAE is dedicated to preserving the record of this progress for others. This book joins many other popular ASAE titles in recording the Exciting developments in agricultural equipment history.

John Deere Tractors Worldwide
A Century of Progress 1893-1993

Editor: Len Lindstrom
Book Designer: Melissa Carpenter
Cover Designer: Bill Thompson

Library of Congress Card Number (LCCN) 94-078879
International Standard Book Number (ISBN) 0-929355-55-5

Copyright © 1994 by the American Society of Agricultural Engineers. All rights reserved. No part of this book may be used or reproduced in any manner without the express written consent of the publisher except in the case of brief quotations embodied in critical reviews or articles about the book. For information address the publisher; the American Society of Agricultural Engineers.

Printed in the U.S.A.

Acknowledgements

The contribution of many people helped in the compiling of *John Deere Tractors Worldwide—A Century of Progress 1893-1993* during the past two years. I was given continued access to the archives in East Moline, and I would like to thank Les Stegh for this major source of photos and other material. Don Huber was again my continual reference contact at Moline H.Q.

In addition, the archives in Mannheim provided many of the European facts, figures, and photos, and my contacts there were Hans Hetterich and his assistant, Christine Nagler. Steve Mitchell of Pharo Communications in the U.K and Jim Purvis at Langar branch house helped with the appendices and photos.

From the rest of the Deere world, photos and information were received from Eloy Galvan Garcia in Spain; Jean-Francois Pierre in France; Alberto Souto, Argentina; Mr. Wills in South Africa; and Danny Keller of the Australian branch. The restored Chamberlain tractor photos and serial number information came from Philip Wyndhan in Western Australia.

The Two-Cylinder Club graciously allowed reproduction of any photos which had appeared in their publications and *Green Magazine* were their usual helpful selves.

Tony Watson, who keeps the worldwide Lanz register, kindly checked that part of the text and accompanying photos.

I express my thanks to many individuals who provided information and photos from all over the world; in particular Bjorn Rockler with information and photos of the Swedish "GMW" tractors, and Dennis Franz for details and pictures of the fascinating model Spoke "D." Many others, too numerous to mention here, I have acknowledged in the captions to their allied tractors.

As in my previous two books, editorial scrutiny was provided by Len Lindstrom. He did his usual job of dotting the i's, crossing the t's, and providing a translation from my English into one the majority of our readers understand.

The team at ASAE, the publisher, deserve a warm note of appreciation for sandwiching work on this book in their normal work load. Melissa Carpenter masterminded the operation with able assistance from Donna Hull, director of marketing. Bill Thompson displayed his artistic talent in the cover design. Sharon McKnight did the difficult tables.

Computers have taken much of the drudgery out of producing a book, but they have not eliminated the need for teamwork. I wish to thank the entire John Deere and ASAE team.

Don Macmillan
August 1994

Introduction

To mark the centenary of the tractor, it has been decided to take an in-depth look at the worldwide spread of the John Deere tractor line from America to Europe, to Central America, and to the Southern Hemisphere.

From the blacksmith's shop of 1837, to becoming the world's largest manufacturer of agricultural machinery in 1963, Deere & Company had always focussed its attention on the home market, and the midwest in particular.

Its full commitment to the tractor in 1918 with the purchase of the Waterloo Gasoline Engine Company meant that it was immediately involved in the export market, with about 4,000 Waterloo Boy tractors going to the British Isles to help with the World War I food effort.

Following the introduction of the Model "D," many of these were exported to Argentina and Russia. A "GPWT" was used by the German Lanz company as a pattern for its first attempt at a row-crop model, and the neighboring markets of Canada and Mexico were a natural outlet for the growing tractor business.

But it was not until the 1950s, under the presidency of Charles Deere Wiman that active steps were taken to consider manufacturing abroad. In 1951 the British Labor government persuaded John Deere and Rolls Royce to build factories in East Kilbride, Scotland, with the promise of a steel allocation in the difficult post-war years. The latter proceeded with their scheme, but Deere withdrew when a change of government altered the agreed terms.

The next investigation in 1953 involved the purchase of Lanz in Germany, whose Mannheim factory had been flattened by allied bombing during World War II, but the board initially decided against.

When William A. (Bill) Hewitt succeeded as President of Deere in 1955, and with Ellwood F. (Woody) Curtis as his running mate on the financial side, a second look was taken at the proposal, and in 1956 at he decision was taken to purchase. The future course of the company as a worldwide manufacturer had been set.

It is the purpose of this volume to chart the progress of this decision as it applies to Deere's tractor line; from the early problems of marrying local tradition with American thinking, extension into France and Spain, and setting up of plants in Mexico and the old-established market in Argentina, the network spread gradually to cover Europe, the Americas, and the Southern Hemisphere.

Today's markets demand a new and developing look at tractor source and manufacture involving cooperation with other companies, from the more competitively priced Eastern European-built Zetor models from the Czech Republic for third world markets, to the alliance with Renault announce Republic for third world markets, to the alliance with Renault announce by the chairman, Hans Becherer, as the period covered by this book comes to an end. Who knows what exciting prospects lie ahead for The Long Green Line.

D.M.

Table of Contents

Part I: Historical Review
Deere Tractors Worldwide—An Initial Survey 2

Waterloo—Deere's World Tractor Center 6
Dreyfuss Styles the Line 9
Deere Commits Worldwide. 13
The Sound-Gard Body 19
Enter the 1980s 23
The U.S. 50 Series. 25
Last of the Australian Line 26
Economy Models Match the Times 26
Record-Breaking Yanmar Line 27
Mannheim's Largest Model Has MFWD As Standard 27
Specialist Models. 28
50 Series for Europe. 28
New Models in South Africa 29
Denver Announcement of Large 60 Series 30
Deere's Largest-Ever Introduction 31
Spain Specializes 32
60 Series Row-Crop Tractors for 1991 33
5000 Series Announced 34
A "New" New Generation 34
A Fourth Model in Updated 70 Series Four-Wheel-Drive Tractors 37
6000 and 7000 Series Extended 38
Around the World in '93. 39
Economy Models from Czech Republic 39

Part II: Product Review
The 2-Cylinder Era, Part 1: 1893-1951 42

The First 30 Years 42
Enter the "D". 44
"D" Variations 48
A Smaller Row-Crop Tractor 50
A 2-Row Alternate 52
Deere's First Orchard Model 54
Hydraulics Replace Mechanical Lift. 56
Standard and Orchard Models Added 60
Lindeman Fills Crawler Niche 62
Horticulture Needs Met 66
Largest Row-Crop Model Introduced. 68

Smallest 2-Cylinder Horizontal Model	70
Models "A" and "B" Modernized	72
New Vertical 2-Cylinder Models from New Factory	74
Deere's First Diesel	76
Dreyfuss Adds Styling	64
Six Speeds Replace Four	64

The 2-Cylinder Era, Part 2: 1952-1960 — 78

A Swedish Compliment?	78
The Numbered Series	78
Dubuque Models Join the Line	80
Deere's First Diesel Row-Crop Model	82
A Power Increase of 20%	84
The Largest 2-Cylinder Tractor	88
Last 2-Cylinder Series Introduced	90
A Small Diesel Model Ends 2-Cylinder Era	94

Multi-Cylinder Models Replace the 2-Cylinder Line — 96

20 Series from Waterloo	100
World Tractor Designed	102
A Smaller Row-Crop Model from Waterloo	102
Small Tractor Line Extended	104
Waterloo Tractors Updated and Line Extended	106
Deere's First Turbocharged Model	108
Super 4020 and New 4620 Greet the 1970s	108
Deere Returns to the 4-Wheel-Drive Market	110
Generation II	112
30 Series Extended	114
Canada Acquires 30 Series from Mannheim	116

New Styling Adopted Worldwide — 118

The 40 Series Utility Line	118
The Japanese Connection	118
The Iron Horses Announced	120
4-Wheel-Drive Models Updated	120
Utility Models Restyled	122
Canada Acquires 40 New Series	122
50 Series Have Caster/Action MFWD Option	124
The Efficiency Experts 45 to 85 Horsepower	124
Other Additions to 50 Series	128
The 55 Series for 1987 and 150th Anniversary	130
Palm Springs New Product Announcement Largest Ever	132

All-New 60 Series Articulated Tractors 134
Under-40-Horsepower Line Extended in 1989 136
Largest 155- to 200-Horsepower Tractors Fine-Tuned to Become 60 Series 138
Augusta Works Built for 5000 Series Production. 138
An All-New Breed of Power. 140
6000 4-Cylinder and 7000 6-Cylinder Models for 1993 140
New 70 Series 4WD Tractors for 1993 142
New 6-Cylinder Models from Waterloo and Mannheim 144

Overseas Beginnings—Germany/France 146

The European Inheritance 146
Final 1-Cylinder Designs Adopt Green and Yellow. 150
Europe's New Generation Models 152
First New Generation European Models Updated. 154
A World Tractor Design 156
30 Series Retains 20 Series Styling. 158
Mannheim Follows Waterloo's New Style 160
40 Series. 162
Large Tractors from Waterloo 166

Further Overseas Developments: Spain, Italy, and Mexico. 178

Spain Joins the Deere Fold 178
Deere's First Spanish Model 180
Spain Announces 20 Series 182
Getafe's 30 Series Announced 184
35 Series Has New Stying 186
Spanish "Schedule Masters" 188
50 Series Introduced and Line Lengthened in 1987 192
A Time of Change. 194
Italian Models Adopted for Small European Farms. 196
Mexico Assembles Waterloo and Mannheim Tractors 198
55 Series Built in Saltillo 200

Southern Hemisphere: Argentina, South Africa, and Australia 202

Argentina's 2-Cylinder Models. 202
20 and 30 Series Built in Rosario 204
40 Series Arrive in 1981 206
Last Rosario Models Still in Production. 208
Imported Models Extend the Argentine Line 210
South Africa—Local 41 Series Introduced in 1982. 212
51 Series Supersedes 41 Series in 1987. 212
Australia and Chamberlain in 1948 216

First of the Champions 218
Third Styling Exercise for 1966 220
Deere Influence Shows in New Series 222
Czech-Zetor 226

Part III: Appendices

A-1 Worldwide Tractor Comparisons, United States, European and Other Equivalents 228
A-2 U.S. Specifications, Waterloo Diesel Tractors 230
A-3 Tractor Specification Augusta, Yanmar, Mannheim, Goldini,
     Satillo, Rosario, Nigel, & Welshpool 231
A-4 U.S. Tractor Specification, U.S.-Mannheim Built Diesel Tractors 234
A-5 Nebraska Tractor Tests, Waterloo Diesel Tractors 235
A-6 Nebraska/OECD Tractor Tests. U.S.-Mannheim Built Diesel Tractors 236
A-7 Tractor Tests, Augusta and Mannheim 237
A-8 Production Years and Serial Numbers 238
A-9 Chamberlain Tractors 240

John Deere Tractors Worldwide
A Century of Progress
1893-1993

Don Macmillan

Deere Tractors Worldwide—An Initial Survey

From the first successful tractor to today's sophisticated machines, John Deere has risen to world leadership in both the farming and lawn and garden care products tractor markets. The international implications and requirements of this position form the subject of this pictorial survey.

Built in seven factories around the world, today's complex and sophisticated John Deere tractors are a far cry from Froelich's steel-wheeled single-cylinder traction unit, which threshed 72,000 bushels of grain in South Dakota in 1892. Progress has taken the tractor from a single speed, forward and reverse, to 24 forward, 16 reverse speeds in a century—the time span of this volume. From the four Froelich tractors produced in 1893 to Mannheim's one millionth, a 6400 in 1993, the one hundred years has seen the growth of Deere into the world's largest manufacturer of farm machinery.

In the beginning was the Froelich, one man's vision of the future, when steam and horses ruled the farming firmament. With lack of fuel supplies for the former in the vast stretches of the Dakotas, Froelich's answer was to mount one of the new internal combustion engines on a steamer's chassis.

The result, according to R. B. Gray (editor of *The Agricultural Tractor 1855-1950*), was the world's first successful tractor. Only four more were built in 1893 and two sold, but both were returned. A different design, with a single-cylinder horizontal engine of the Waterloo company's own make, was built and sold in 1896 and another similar one in 1897.

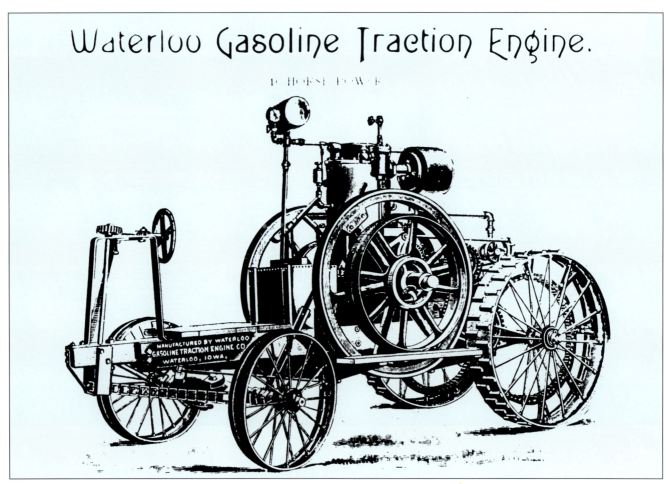

Reproduced from the original sales brochure of 1893, this line drawing was used by the Waterloo Gasoline Traction Engine Co. to advertise their new reversible Froelich tractor.

One of the oldest surviving Waterloo Boy Model "R" series G tractors, No. 1,568, with headless engine, owned by Travis Jorde of Rochester and decalcomania fame. Note the right-side position of the radiator, which was soon altered to the left to give the operator a clearer view forward; also note the small-diameter dual-fuel tank for gasoline and kerosene.

But these early tractors were ahead of their time; it was 1912 before the Waterloo Gasoline Engine Company again entered the tractor field. The 1912 Waterloo Boy 25-horsepower Standard model with 4-cylinder cross-mounted engine was followed in 1913 by the "Sure Grip, Never Slip" with the same basic layout but with crawler tracks instead of rear wheels, and the Models "C" and "H." All four had production records which were lost in the mists of time. Then came the "L/LA," 29 of which were recorded sold in early 1914. This latter model had a 2-cylinder horizontally opposed kerosene-burning engine and was available in 3- and 4-wheel modes.

It was soon replaced by the very successful Model "R," with over 8,000 units built between 1914 and 1918, and still in production when Deere took over the company in March 1918. This model adopted the horizontal 2-cylinder side-by-side engine which was to stay with John Deere until 1960 in the States and 1970 in Argentina.

In 1917 the final version of the Waterloo Boy was introduced, the two-speed Model "N," and would stay in production with modifications until Deere's first Waterloo-built tractor, the famous Model "D," appeared in 1923. From 1912 to 1918, Deere experimented with both a tractor and a motor cultivator, and in 1918 actually produced 100 All-Wheel-Drive models in East Moline. However, they were too sophisticated and expensive for the farmers of that time, so they were dropped in favor of the simpler 2-cylinder concept.

In Europe the Lanz company, which was to become part of the Deere empire in 1956, produced its first tractor, the Model LB "Landbaumotor" in 1911. Updates followed in 1914 with the LC, in 1917 with the LCM, and from 1919 to 1926 with the LD I, II, and III. The most significant development for Deere, however, took place in 1921 with the introduction of the first Bulldog crude-oil tractor, examples of which can be found in both the Mannheim and Moline archives.

On the day when the one millionth tractor produced in the Mannheim factory came off the line, the first Bulldog from the works museum was brought over in honor of the occasion. Hans Hetterich, manager marketing services, is at the controls, while the Mannheim Works general manager, Hannes Kremkau, leans on the 6400's fender.

Deere Tractors Worldwide—An Initial Survey

The largest example of the last series of Bulldog tractors, this 65-hp Model D6516 was built in the Lanz Iberica works in Getafe, near Madrid, Spain, in the late 1950s.

The manufacture of Deere tractors spread to Europe in 1956. It continued its worldwide expansion with the opening of the Rosario factory in Argentina in 1958, followed in 1959 by Monterrey, Mexico, where implements had been built since 1954. In Spain, Deere finally acquired majority control in 1961 of the Lanz Iberica Getafe factory, originally opened in 1956, when the latest Lanz single-cylinder models were produced.

The 4-cylinder Model 505, a Deere-designed update of the original New Generation Model 500 built in Mannheim, was introduced in August 1963 at the first Deere dealer convention in Spain, after the investment of several hundred million pesetas in tooling and machinery. This was followed in 1966 by four 10-series models: the 515, 515V, 717, and 818.

With Mannheim-designed tractors as their basis, Getafe gradually became the manufacturer of specialist types for orchards, vineyards, and crops requiring extra-high clearance, leaving the standard types to Mannheim. The introduction in 1987 of some Italian Goldoni-built models was again largely for orchard and vineyard use.

Mexico is another Spanish-speaking country to build tractors. Initially assembling U.S. designed 435, 630, 730, and 830 models, followed by the Waterloo New Generation tractors, the factory in Monterrey added the smaller 1020, 2020, and 2120 before introducing its 35 series in 1973. Ten years later the 55 series were introduced, built in the newly refurbished ex-International Harvester factory in Saltillo.

In the southern hemisphere, South Africa joined the countries building Deere machinery in 1968. It expanded into tractors in 1981, when Mannheim models were fitted with locally built ADE engines, as required by the South African government.

In Mexico this 4435 Turbo tractor is seen disking with locally built MX428 disks. The tractors supplied were mostly of the open-station type as shown.

Argentina had always been a good market for the company's tractors, so it was not surprising that in 1958 a factory was built in Rosario to first assemble and then build the Waterloo 2-cylinder Model 730 in four versions. These were followed by the local version of the U.S. Model 435, called the 445, and again in four different models. It was 1970 before these 2-cylinder tractors gave way to the 20 series multi-cylinder models, which have since been followed by the Mannheim 30, 40, and 50 series.

The Australian Chamberlain Company experimented with tractors before World War II, and introduced the 40K 2-cylinder horizontally opposed model in 1946, starting production in 1948. Following some years of association with Deere, the company became wholly owned in 1970, and continued building models in Welshpool suitable for local conditions.

The latest move in the expansion of the company's tractor line was the opening in 1991 of a new factory in Augusta, Georgia, to build the 5000 series 3-cylinder models. With the introduction of the 4- and now 6-cylinder 6000 series from Mannheim and the 7000 6-cylinder series from Waterloo, all the tractors available are now being standardized worldwide.

The Waterloo-designed 730 two-cylinder models were first assembled, and later built, in Rosario. They were offered as both standard and row-crop models with twin-wheel or wide-front-end axles, or Hi-Crop. Note the Argentinian variation of the medallion, and the shell fenders.

Fitted with a 40-hp two-cylinder horizontally opposed all-fuel engine, the first Chamberlain tractors appeared in 1946, their launch having been delayed by the war. A restored production Model 40K is shown at a rally in Australia, with a later 55KA behind.

Deere Tractors Worldwide—An Initial Survey

Waterloo—Deere's World Tractor Center

Waterloo is the world center of this extensive development. The Waterloo Gasoline Traction Engine Company was organized on January 10, 1893, to produce the first successful internal combustion traction engine with John Froelich, its designer, as president. The initial company only lasted until November 18, 1895, due to the lack of tractor sales, and was replaced on that day by the Waterloo Gasoline Engine Company to continue producing stationary engines, though without its founder president, whose primary interest was in tractors.

The original 12 engine models were rationalized in 1905 to six, rated from 2 to 12 horsepower and took the name Waterloo Boy. It was another six years before the company again entered the tractor market, first with a large Standard 25-horsepower Model "TP," followed by the "Sure Grip, Never Slip" crawler version and further smaller Models "C," "H," and "L" or Light Tractor.

Both single- and two-speed models are shown in this photo taken at a vintage show near Oxford, England: respectively, Model "R," style E, Serial No. 4,779, and Model "N," Serial No. 19,952. The latter is restored in Waterloo Boy colors, although both tractors are in fact Overtimes.

Production numbers of the first four Waterloo Boy tractors are not known, but 29 Model "L" 3-wheel and the similar 4-wheel "LA" tractors were built and sold in early 1914. As with the Models "C" and "H," these tractors had 2-cylinder horizontally opposed kerosene-burning engines.

Early in 1914, experiments were instigated to produce a twin-cylinder type and in June 1914 the first Model "R," style A, appeared followed by 11 more styles. The last, style M, was still in production when Deere acquired the company on March 14, 1918. The "R" had a single forward and reverse speed and over 8,000 were produced in the four years, many being exported to the United Kingdom to assist with World War I food-production effort. L. J. Martin, who imported these, called his company the Overtime Tractor Company, and the tractors thus acquired the name Overtime.

The first Waterloo Boy Light Tractors were equipped with a two-cylinder horizontally opposed 15-hp engine. Only 29 of this model were built before the change during 1914 to the Model "R" with its 25-hp twin side-by-side engine.

6

No spoke-flywheel Model "D" tractors were imported originally into England, but one or two have since found their way across the ocean. These two were at the first U.K. EXPO at Wood Green Show, Huntingdon in 1992. The 26-in. model, Serial No. 31,030, is the only example of this model to date, the 24-in tractor, Serial No. 34,628, is the author's.

In 1917 a new Model "N" was introduced, with 2-speed forward, 1-reverse enclosed gearbox, but the same engine as the last "R." This had been increased in size from the original 5.5-inch bore, 7-inch stroke to 6-inch bore from style H and to 6.5 inches with the last style M. The "R" was phased out by Deere but the "N" continued in production into 1924, and beyond the advent of their first 2-cylinder design, the famous Model "D," which appeared in 1923.

The Waterloo company inaugurated experimental work prior to the Deere take-over in an effort to overcome the wear experienced with the external final drive gears. The first model in 1917 proved unsatisfactory, but the adoption of chains for the final drives in 1918 overcame the main problem.

In 1923 the first 50 Model "D" tractors had four openings in the radiator sides, a fabricated front axle, and different letter styling on the radiator top tank from that adopted later.

Some 879 of the tractors fitted with 26-inch spoke flywheels were produced before a change was made to 24-inch diameter with a jointed steering rod. In October 1925 a PTO shaft was offered as special equipment, but it was July 1927, when the first major update occurred with the increase in cylinder bore from 6.5 to 6.75 inches—the size used until the last "D" was made in 1953. A splined flywheel replaced the previous keyed type.

Other major changes made to the "D" were the introduction of right-side worm and gear steering in November 1930, a third forward gear late in 1934, and the styling introduced in 1939.

By 1926 the need for a tractor smaller than the "D," one with row-crop capability, became obvious and experiments began. The result was five tractors of varying configuration, with a 4-wheel 3-row design going into production in 1927, the Model "C." Almost all of the tractors built that year were recalled for factory modifications, and 52 were reissued as the Model "GP" or general purpose, since the letters C and D were easily confused when ordering.

The first tractor to be fitted with four methods of transmitting its power, through the belt pulley, drawbar, PTO, and a mechanical lift, was the 3-row row-crop Model "C." Its successor, the "GP," was offered in different guises.

The Kellers' Model "C," Serial No. 200,109, unlike most of the first batch of these tractors, was never rebuilt, but retained its original serial number. Doug Kiel's 1941 Stearman biplane makes a suitable background at the opening of the Two-Cylinder Club's new Grundy Center, Iowa, headquarters.

Deere Tractors Worldwide—An Initial Survey

There was still a requirement for a 2-row tractor in some states, so the original design was adapted and announced as the "GPWT" or wide-tread. In Maine the potato growers were offered a narrow version of this, the Model "P," while fruit growers had the option of the "GPO" and a few of the latter were fitted with tracks by Lindeman in the state of Washington.

But the "GP" was soon to be eclipsed by a new model, the "A," which replaced the mechanical lift with hydraulic lift. With increased visibility due to a tapered hood (which had first been tried on the final "GPWT" design), twin front and easily adjusted rear wheels, the "A" quickly became the farmer's favorite.

It was followed within a year by a smaller version, the Model "B," and both sizes were offered shortly after in various modes as single-wheel or wide-axle front, high-crop, standard tread, orchard, and industrial models.

Another line of tractors was developed in Moline in 1936 with an experimental 2-cylinder vertical all-gas engine. This Model "Y" was followed with production tractors first designated Model 62, but soon after called the Model "L." In

The first production unstyled Model "B," Serial No. 1,000, is now in the collection of Walter and Bruce Keller in Wisconsin.

its final form the "L" was increased from 10 to 14 horsepower and became the "LA." Initially unstyled, these tractors received the styling treatment ultimately given to the whole line by Henry Dreyfuss.

This open-fanshaft Model "A" seen at Bob Schreiber's in Milo, Iowa, has a four-bolt front column and steering wheel with center casting as fitted to the first "A" tractors.

Another example of the Keller collection, Model 62, Serial No. 621,023, heads the lineup which greeted the author on his first visit to their place in Wisconsin in June 1982.

A nicely restored "H," Serial No. 36,599, fitted with electric starting and lights, arrives for the first U.K. Two-Cylinder Club EXPO.

Dreyfuss Styles the Line

The "A" and "B" were the first models so treated by Dreyfuss, followed by the Models "D" and "L." The orchard version of the Model "A" had been streamlined in 1936 and is commonly known as the "AOS," but this was a pre-Dreyfuss exercise.

Demand for more power by row-crop farmers prompted the introduction of the "G" in 1937, but only in twin-front-wheel form. It was during 1938 when Waterloo completed its line of tractors with the smallest of their horizontal 2-cylinder designs, the "H." Production began for the "H" in 1939 in styled form, although experimental models had been built unstyled. Other models had to wait for their update. A single-front-wheel option was offered, and for one year only, two high-crop versions, the "HNH" single-wheel and "HWH" wide-front, tractors of both styles that generally went to California. Some of the later Model "H" tractors were equipped with electric starting and lighting.

The "G" was the first of the remaining unstyled models to receive the Dreyfuss treatment in 1941. The opportunity was taken for a further update with the provision of six forward gears to replace the old 4-speed box, and optional electric starting and lighting.

Accordingly, Deere wanted to increase the price, but was prevented from doing so by government controls. As a result the model name was changed to "GM" or "G modernized," although the serial numbers remained in sequence and showed on the plate as G-13,000 up.

Recently it has been learned that as soon as restrictions were lifted at the end of the war, the "GM" reverted to "G" (Serial No. 23,000 up), but continued for nearly 3,000 more examples with the GM-style pan seat and battery position. It finally received the armchair seat with battery beneath, as used on the later Models "A" and "B," from Serial No. 26,000.

One of the postwar Model "G" tractors built to the same specifications as the wartime "GM," and before the change to armchair seat with batteries below. This tractor, Serial No. 24,640, is equipped with optional electric starting and lighting.

Deere Tractors Worldwide—An Initial Survey

The Model "M" tractors were never imported to the U.K. Several examples were sent to Southern Ireland. The first one to be introduced to England by the author, in 1962, Serial No. 14,021, is shown above. It remained in his collection for 26 years until 1988, and was latterly on loan to the British Science Museum.

The "BR" and "BO" were never styled but the latter was fitted with crawler tracks by Lindeman in Yakima, Washington, to satisfy a demand in the West for this type of unit in hilly orchards. This application was of sufficient interest to Deere for them to acquire the factory in 1946 and continue building the "BO"-Lindeman.

In 1947 a new factory was built in Dubuque, Iowa, to produce the new Model "M." This was a 2-cylinder all-gasoline vertical-engined tractor designed to replace the "L," "LA," and "H" series and to compete in the marketplace with the small grey Ferguson. With the later "MT" tricycle version and the "MC" crawler replacement for the "BO"-Lindeman, it proved a popular second tractor on many farms, though it lacked the three-point linkage and sensing of the competition.

The "AR" and "AO" were the last of the prewar models to be styled in 1949. They adopted a new styling first used that same year on Deere's first diesel 2-cylinder tractor, the Model "R." The aging "D," excellent as it had proved over its 30-year lifetime, was no longer powerful enough for new farming demands and the "R" proved to be the answer.

Its diesel engine was started with a 2-cylinder horizontally opposed gasoline engine allowing preheating of the main motor. The gasoline engine was started electrically. With a 5-speed transmission and remote hydraulic outlets, the "R" was master of all grain farming requirements in the early 1950s.

Just prior to the introduction of the "R," the first prototype Chamberlain tractors (also 2-cylinder models, but initially with kerosene-burning horizontally opposed engines) had appeared in Australia in 1946. Production started in 1948 and a diesel version, the 55DA, with the same basic style engine was announced in 1954, having been preceded by a few GM 2-cycle 3-cylinder diesel 60DA tractors in 1952-53.

The only Model "R" imported originally into the British Isles, Serial No. 4,661, was imported into Dublin by the concessionaires Jack Olding in 1950. It was brought to England with the Model "M" shown above, and both are now the property of Graham Ellis of Chagford, Devon.

John Deere's first diesel row-crop tractor was the Model 70 introduced in 1953. This 70RC, Serial No. 33,877, was shown at the first Two-Cylinder Club EXPO in Waterloo, Iowa, in 1987.

From 1955 Chamberlain relied chiefly on Perkins 4- and 6-cylinder engines until 1975 when, following the merger with Deere in 1970, the Champion 239 was equipped with a Deere 4-cylinder 4-239 unit.

At home in the States the 2-cylinder models were updated in 1952 with the introduction of the first of the numbered series, the 50 and 60 replacing the "B" and "A." The following year the 40 series replaced the "M" line and the 70 replaced the "G." It was not, however, until 1955 that this series was completed, with the 80 replacing the very popular Model "R."

Deere's first diesel row-crop tractor, the Model 70, was announced in 1953 and its 2-cylinder diesel was started with a new V-4 gasoline engine in place of the 2-cylinder horizontally opposed unit of the "R." When the latter was in turn replaced by the 80, it too had the new starting engine.

The Model 55DA was one of the early 2-cylinder horizontally opposed diesel models built by Chamberlain in Welshpool, Australia, in 1954.

Deere Tractors Worldwide—An Initial Survey

With farmers demanding increased power, the whole series horsepower was increased about 20 percent, and the result was the introduction of the 20 series. At the smaller end of the line a new model, the 320, was effectively the 40 continued; the rest with increased power became the 420 thru 820. The first 420 models from Dubuque were all green, but these soon received the yellow hood panel adopted by Waterloo.

Two years later the whole tractor line became the 30 series, but these tractors retained the same engine dimensions, making retesting at Nebraska unnecessary. Their new styling gave some indication of changes that would become standard in 1960.

Perhaps Daniel O'Brien of Barnet, Vermont, in a *Green Magazine* article put it best:

"I studied them (the 30 series) for hours, my eyes transfixed by the sensually pleasing green and yellow hoods with the characteristic slant down the sides. The rounded front grill and dual headlight fenders gave the tractors a finished look like a highly polished emerald."

"The styling of the 30 series was just plain eye catching, everything 'fit' was correct in proportion. Deere was well aware of the aesthetic enhancements that came from the upgrade from 20 to 30 series tractors. It was the last hurrah to a phenomenal engineering marvel that spanned parts of five decades. Deere paid tribute, literally, to the two cylinders by allowing them to enter the slip stream of history in style".

A nicely restored example of the 720 diesel standard tractor owned by Robert Carrico of Madison, Kentucky, represents the 20 series.

None of the numbered series of 2-cylinder tractors were exported to the U.K. due to government financial restrictions, but this 830, Serial No. 2,719, found its way to Norfolk, England, in 1990 and has been beautifully restored by its owner, David Lee of Hunstanton.

Deere Commits Worldwide

The beginning of John Deere's commitment to the worldwide vision it holds today was first evident with the purchase of the Lanz Company in Germany in 1956. Lanz was a company with a history almost as old as Deere's. The company had been founded in 1859 and had built both stationary and mobile steam engines from the end of the nineteenth century.

In 1912 it produced its first "agricultural engine," the Landbaumotor, and continued this line of development until 1925. The most significant step, however, was taken in 1921 with the announcement of the first crude-oil tractor in the world, the famous Bulldog. This first tractor was rated at 12 horsepower. In 1923 a 4-wheel-drive version appeared with pivot steering and the same engine.

The Bulldog line was developed through the hopper-cooled Gross-Bulldog HR2 22/28-horsepower models in 1926. The similar-powered radiator-cooled Model HR4 was introduced in 1928, followed by a multiplicity of models through to the 19 sizes of single-cylinder diesels in the line when Deere acquired the company on November 12, 1956.

This number was reduced to 13 within a year and to 11 by 1959. The last significant single-cylinder design of the German Lanz Bulldog era, the 40-horsepower D4016, was announced in 1957.

Having acquired the green and yellow finish in 1958, the Bulldog era ended in Germany in 1960 with the introduction of Europe's New Generation models in January of that year. Together with Lanz in Germany, Deere had acquired an interest in Lanz Ibérica, Spain, where some of the Bulldog models were built from 1956 until as late as 1963.

In 1958 a factory was built in Rosario, Argentina, to assemble the 730 diesel 2-cylinder Waterloo tractor in four styles—standard, tricycle, wide-front, and high-crop. It was to be another six years before the smaller 445, the Argentine version of the U.S. 435, was announced, again in five styles—row-crop utility,

Part of the comprehensive collection owned by Eric Barker of Westhorpe, Suffolk, England, this nice Lanz Bulldog D4016, Serial No. 345,967, is in its original green and yellow livery.

In 1964 the Rosario Works in Argentina started building the Model 445, their version of the U.S. 435. Shown is the row-crop utility model. Other types included an economy version, a twin-front-wheel tricycle, an orchard, and a narrow vineyard model, none of which had appeared in the United States.

an economy version, tricycle, orchard, and vineyard, none of the latter four having appeared in the States.

Also in 1958 the factory in Monterrey, Mexico, which had been building implements since it was opened in 1954, started assembling tractors. The first models chosen were the Waterloo 630, 730, and 830 2-cylinder tractors.

Deere Tractors Worldwide—An Initial Survey

Ken Becker from Hartington, Nebraska, was the lucky owner of the first 3010 and 4010 diesel tractors built, both carrying the Serial No. 1,000.

As 1960 dawned, the John Deere tractor world, indeed the whole tractor world, would never be quite the same again. To the initial despair of the lovers of the 1- and particularly the 2-cylinder concept, multi-cylinder tractors became the order of the day. The new 10 series, especially those built in Waterloo, revolutionized the farmer's ability to cover critical operations at optimum times.

The 4-cylinder 3010 and 6-cylinder 4010 and 5010 were quickly accepted as a giant leap forward in farm mechanization, and the plows and cultivators designed to match their capabilities enhanced this popularity. With one announcement Deere put itself 10 years ahead of the competition.

The models produced in Dubuque were the 36-horsepower 1010 and the 46-horsepower 2010 in various configurations.

Studio line-up of the New Generation 10 series gasoline tractors—the tricycle 4010, 3010, and 2010, and the standard 1010.

As with the New Generation models in America, Henry Dreyfuss was responsible for the styling of the first John Deere models to be produced in the Mannheim factory in Germany. Shown are the mock-ups for the 100 (nearest camera), 300, and 500 introduced in January 1960. Note that only the 300 has an engine in this photo.

Mannheim had anticipated the New Generation announcement in August 1960 in the States by introducing its 300 and 500 models in January of that year. If one is impartial the models produced in both Dubuque and Mannheim did not achieve the same degree of success as those from Waterloo, and it was not until the 20 series "World Tractor" line was introduced that truly comparable models were available for the smaller farm operation.

This classic 4020, Serial No. 263,524, is restored as originally supplied. Although row-crop wide-front models, they were equipped with standard-type fenders in Europe. Both Power Shift, as in this case, and Syncro-Range transmissions were optional.

Three years later a facelift was given to the original series of 100, 300, 500, and 700 by introducing a 10 series with increased power, but these retained the German 10-speed transmission and U.S. 10 series engines. Europe also had to await the introduction of Mannheim-built 1020 and 2020 tractors before it had a really satisfactory smaller size tractor.

France had been added to the countries with Deere manufacturing facilities when the company became involved in 1959 with a marketing cooperative of three French companies specializing in forage, hay, and harvesting machines, the Compagnie Continentale de Motoculture or C.C.M. With this entry to the French market a new engine factory was planned, and a site bought at Saran near Orleans in 1962 to build Dubuque designed engines for European tractors and harvesting machines.

The U.S. and export markets received a further boost in 1963 with the introduction of the 3020 and 4020 row-crop tractors. Available with a Power Shift transmission and an optional power differential lock, these machines had considerably better performance than the previous 10 series.

Deere Tractors Worldwide—An Initial Survey

In the same year, 1963, Deere held their first dealer convention in Spain and introduced the first model of their own design. The 505 was similar to the Mannheim-built 500, but with an English-built Standard engine.

In 1965 Waterloo announced a smaller tricycle row-crop tractor, the 2510, fitted with the new Dubuque 4-cylinder engine shortly to be announced in the new 2020 tractor, larger of the two new 20 series utility tractors from that factory. The 2510 was offered with either gasoline, diesel, or LP engine and twin-wheel, single-wheel, or wide front axles as with the larger models, and as a Hi-Crop model in addition.

When they were announced late in 1965 the 1020 and 2020 were no longer available in tricycle form, but could be purchased as low LU, regular RU, or high HU models. They were designed as part of a plan for a worldwide tractor, with many options including power steering and differential lock like the larger models, plus the choice of three rear and one mid-mounted PTO. An 8-speed constant-mesh transmission was standard.

The year 1966 saw the 5010 updated to 5020, but more significant for the future was the introduction of the Roll-Gard rollover protective structure (ROPS). This design was subsequently

The second series of John Deere-designed models built in Getafe were made in three sizes and four models, the standard 515, 717, and 818, and the vineyard version of the 515V.

made available free to all competitors, emphasizing Deere's commitment to safety. In the same year the Lanz name was dropped in all markets.

Production began in the French Saran works in 1963 with the assembly of three models based on Mannheim designs, the vineyard model 303V and the orchard models 303F and 505F. Engine production for the 30 series Zweibrucken combines began in 1965, and in 1967 the new 3- and 4-cylinder engines for the 20 series tractors were introduced.

In 1967, John Deere Iberica SA in Spain was formed. The factory in Getafe, near Madrid, built a further series of tractors developed from the Mannheim models, the 515 and 515V (45 hp), 717 (56 hp), and 818 (60 hp).

In Europe, 1968 saw the introduction of five sizes of 20 series tractors: the 3-cylinder 820 (34 hp), 920 (40 hp), 1020 (47 hp), 1120 (52 hp), and the 4-cylinder 2020 (64 hp). The 1020-V was offered as a vineyard model, and the 1020-O and 2020-O for orchard work.

This studio picture of 1020 and 2020 tractors with Roll-Gard ROPS was taken in April 1966. The 1020 is a regular RU model, the 2020 the LU low version, hence the difference in height of their hoods.

As was customary in Europe, the new 70-hp 2120 was supplied with a fender passenger seat. The tractor shown has the optional downswept exhaust.

That same year, the 2120 (70 hp) was added to the European line, while the smaller 820 and intermediate size 1520, similar to Europe's 1120 and both built in Mannheim, were added to the U.S. line—an indication of the future.

Also in 1968, the 5020 was uprated from 132 to 143 horsepower and safety cabs were introduced incorporating Roll-Gard ROPS and included air-conditioning, heaters, and a hydraulic control console. Other innovations were Power Front-Wheel Drive and a power weight-transfer hitch.

In Australia the last 2-cylinder tractors were built in 1957. Chamberlain expanded their line, first by fitting the 3-cylinder GM diesel in the Models 60DA (1952) with the original IH-type styling. The Super 70 (1954) was the first model with their second styling, and in 1963 came the Super 90.

Further models were developed over the next seven years, including the introduction of models with adjustable axles for row-crop work and 6-cylinder tractors to meet the demand for extra power. Most models were equipped with Perkins engines, even after Deere took a major interest in the company, until the Champion model was fitted with a 4-cylinder Deere 239-cubic-inch engine in 1975.

While these developments had been taking place on the other side of the world, in the States the 2510 was replaced late in 1968 with the 2520 with similar wheel options. Two other models were introduced, the 4000 was a low-priced version of the 4020. More important was the introduction of the 4520, which was Deere's first tractor with factory-installed turbocharger. It developed 122 horsepower, and was the granddaddy of a long and continuing line of turbocharged tractors.

Chamberlain's second styling exercise is illustrated in this March 1993 photo of a Super 90 at the Bendigo rally in Australia. Lanz tractors are also popular with collectors in Australia.

First of the turbocharged Waterloo models was the 4520, a chunky version of the popular 4020 which found instant favor in both the corn and wheat belts.

17

Deere Tractors Worldwide—An Initial Survey

The 1420 was the smallest of the four 20 series tractors built in the Rosario factory from 1970.

At the same time the 3020 and 4020 were updated with new cylinder block, piston and ring design, dry air cleaner, and the option of Power Front-Wheel Drive. These models are distinguished from the earlier ones by their oval mufflers and are known as the Classic 3020 and 4020.

The European tractor scene was also extended in 1969 with the introduction of Mannheim's first 6-cylinder tractor, the 3120, a real workhorse filling the gap between the local and U.S. imported models. By this time The Long Green Line was lengthening in Europe.

The final disappearance of the much-loved 2-cylinder horizontal engine occurred in 1970 when the Argentine factory stopped building the 730 series and announced the 3-cylinder 1420 (43 hp), 4-cylinder 2420 (66 hp), and 6-cylinder 3420 (77 hp) and 4420 (101 hp) models. The three larger tractors were based on the Classic 3020 and 4020 Waterloo models, the 1420 on the Mannheim 1120.

The 1970s were to see an even longer Long Green Line in the United States with Waterloo announcing in 1971 the 4320, a turbocharged version of the 4020, and at the same time replacing the 4520 with the 135-horsepower 4620, which was intercooled as well as turbocharged.

Deere's reentry into the manufacture of large articulated tractors with the 7020 was anticipated with the introduction of the Wagner WA14 and WA17 in 1969; they were given Deere styling and filled the gap until the new model appeared, but the 7020 was pure Waterloo design. It had the same engine as the 4620.

Its larger stablemate, the 7520 with a 175-horsepower intercooled and turbocharged engine, followed in 1972. This allowed the 5020's successor to be offered with either the 7020 or 7520 engine; the resulting model, the first with an engine option in the company's history, was designated 6030, but retained the 20 series styling, as did another new model, the 60-horsepower 2030 which replaced the 54-horsepower 2020. The 2030 was the last Deere model tested at Nebraska with a gasoline engine.

In 1971 a visit to the Rousseau works in Orleans, France, and the newly opened engine works in Saran produced a first for the author with an opportunity to drive one of the new articulated 7020 tractors shown above.

The Sound-Gard Body

The company took its next giant leap forward with the announcement of the Sound-Gard body for the Waterloo-built tractors in the fall of 1972. The new 30 series were expected to sell in the ratio 40/60 with this new cab, but actually more than three quarters of customers opted for the enclosed air-conditioned unit. In Europe it was standard equipment.

In addition to the new cab, a completely new styling was adopted which again took some getting used to by followers of the green and yellow line. The 4030, 4230, 4430, and 4630 were offered initially, rated from 80 to 150 PTO horsepower. Syncro-Range transmission with a new Perma-Clutch was standard, with another innovation, a 16-speed Quad-Range transmission, as an option. This was a merger of Syncro-Range and the Hi-Lo of the smaller tractors. The three larger models continued with the popular Power Shift of their predecessors available as an option.

To bring the new line to Europe, the largest gathering to that date of dealers, their staffs, and company personnel were joined by the whole Deere & Company board—for the first time in Europe—at Saarbrucken in Germany.

The presentation of the new Sound-Gard-bodied tractors was arranged on screen, with the presenter talking from within the cab, in background silence, into his microphone. At the conclusion he opened the cab door, and one can still hear the gasp of the audience when they realized the tractor had been running all the time!

At the same introduction, new 30 series utility tractors built in Mannheim were announced—the 4-cylinder 71-horsepower 2030 and 79-horsepower 2130 and the 6-cylinder 97-horsepower 3130, all retaining the 20 series styling.

A new 4230 with Sound-Gard body and optional Power Front-Wheel Drive is outside the author's dealership in Devizes, Wiltshire, England.

The smaller models in this series from Mannheim were continued, but vineyard and orchard models were added, 920-V and 1020-V, and 1020-O and 2030-O. The following year the 3-cylinder 59-horsepower 1630 was an addition to the line, and vineyard and orchard versions were also available. They too retained the earlier styling.

In Mexico the 4435 Turbo 6-cylinder tractor, without the refinement of the American Sound-Gard body or Roll-Gard ROPS, was introduced in 1973, followed by the 4235.

The following year saw the last of the earlier styled tractors introduced in the United States, the Mannheim-built 3-cylinder 35-horsepower 830 and 45-horsepower 1530 and Dubuque's 4-cylinder 70-horsepower 2630. The latter was the largest utility tractor built there. Replacing Waterloo's 2520, it indicated the way utility models would develop in the future. All the above were marketed as low-priced tractors in comparison with the opposition.

Deere Tractors Worldwide—An Initial Survey

The 1975 line of five tractor models in Argentina: the 2330 52-hp, 2530 67-hp, 2730 78-hp, 3530 101-hp, and 4530 114-hp, a mix of Mannheim and Waterloo-based designs.

The styling introduced by Waterloo in 1972 became standard in the States in 1975 when the 4-wheel-drive models were replaced with the Sound-Gard-bodied 178-horsepower 8430 and 225-horsepower 8630. Adopted at the same time for the complete line in Europe, this had worldwide repercussions. Argentina introduced their 30 series 2330, 2530, 2730, 3530, and 4530, the 3330 was added in 1977, while Mexico extended its line with the 2535 and 2735 in addition to the two larger models mentioned previously.

A lower-cost cab was introduced in Europe, known as OPU or Operator's Protection Unit, but fully covered the safety and sound requirements for that market. Initially available on the 3130, it was later offered on the 2130, then the 2030, and finally models down to the 1030.

In addition to the new models in Argentina and Mexico, Deere's deepening involvement with Chamberlain was reflected in the announcement of five new models.

In 1975 the 80 series appeared with Deere engines and an all-new distinctly John Deere look, similar to the U.S. industrial models. Chamberlain's new yellow and black color scheme added to this impression.

These models remained, with minor modifications made to become the 80B series, until 1985, when the last tractor line to be built in Welshpool, the 90 series, was introduced. The 90 series was now resplendent in green and yellow but still under the Chamberlain name and trademark. After 1986 it was decided to discontinue tractor manufacture in Australia and import models from Waterloo and Mannheim.

In 1975 the Chamberlain tractor line was completely redesigned and restyled. The color scheme was changed from orange to yellow, giving the tractors a John Deere industrial look, emphasized by the square nose. This 4480 is seeding with an Australian-built Mk2 seeder.

An 1830 with the original styling and ROPS is ready in the yard to go planting with a 7000 planter.

This field view of the new-styled 1830, similarly equipped with ROPS, looks altogether more chunky than its predecessor.

The next major development took place in the United States in 1976 with the restyling of the utility tractor line, introduced as the 40 series. The three smaller, 2040, 2240, and 2440, were built in Mannheim but the 2640 continued from Dubuque. The 2240 was offered in both vineyard and orchard modes.

Since Canada obtained all its utility tractors from Mannheim, the model numbers had always followed Europe. The 2030 in the earlier styling was called the 1830 when shipped to Canada, to avoid confusion with the U.S. 2030, and remained so named when the new style was adopted in Canada. The 1830 was Canada's equivalent of the 2630 and 2640 in the States, but it had a turbocharged 239-cubic-inch 66-horsepower engine, compared with the American naturally aspirated 266-cubic-inch in the latter two.

In Spain the 30 series became the 35 series in 1977, with specifications suitable for that market. Models produced were the 1035, 1635, 2035, 2135, and 3135. They were similar to the new-look 30 series marketed elsewhere. A mechanical 4-wheel drive was offered as an option.

Late in 1977 the New Iron Horses, the 40 series from Waterloo, were announced. With their introduction the models were increased to five in number, from the 90-horsepower 4040 to the new top-of-the-line 180-horsepower 4840. Demand had been for a Sound-Gard-bodied 6030, and the 4840 was designed to fill this need. Thus the days of the large standard 2-wheel-drive tractor had come to an end in The Long Green Line.

Power of all models had been increased, but more significant was the increase of 14 to 29 percent in the hitch lifting capacity. The extra power was matched by an increase in weight or more "iron," hence the name given them.

This 2035 from the Spanish Getafe factory sports the new styling and optional mechanical new front-wheel drive.

Deere Tractors Worldwide—An Initial Survey

The first 6-cylinder model to be imported from Mannheim for the American market was the 80-hp 2840.

With the increase in power of the 4040, the gap between it and the 2640 had widened, thus allowing the introduction of the first 6-cylinder 80-horsepower 2840 from Mannheim with its 12-speed transmission including Hi-Lo as standard.

Another major occurrence in 1977 was Deere's agreement with Yanmar of Japan, that country's second largest tractor maker, to build under-40-horsepower tractors for the U.S. market. At the time, most of the American tractor manufacturers had reached the same conclusion, that it was cheaper to build these smaller models in Japan, with its large home market for this size.

As a result of this agreement, the 22.5-horsepower 850 and 27-horsepower 950 were announced the following year. At the other end of the scale a $1 million consignment of large tractors and combines was sold to China.

In Europe both small and large new models were introduced, the 3-cylinder 32-horsepower 830 and the 6-cylinder 3030, a derated 3130. The 1630 and 2030 were now offered in Hi-Crop or Multi-Crop form, but a development of far-reaching importance was the introduction in Europe of the 1030 to 2030 with a mechanical front-wheel drive option. The 2130 thru 3130 retained the hydrostatic Power Front-Wheel Drive available on the Waterloo models.

Although a new tractor factory was opened in Venezuela in 1978 to assemble Waterloo tractors, by 1980 it had to be closed due to the economic downturn in that country, after a throughput of only 3,200 machines.

Late in 1979 for the 1980 season Mannheim introduced the 40 series, known as the Schedule Masters, from the 840 to the 3140 plus a European-assembled 4040. The occasion was taken to extend the MFWD option from the 1040 to the 3140, and all these models were offered with the OPU cab. Getafe changed over to the new series at the same time.

During that time in the United States the 40 series tractors were updated with a new top-shaft-synchronized transmission option (TSS) and MFWD on the Mannheim-built 2040 and 2240. All models had the 8-speed collar-shift as standard, while the 2040, 2240, and 2640 could also be supplied with either Hi-Lo or a hydraulic direction reverser, giving four optional transmissions on the two smaller models.

One of the first two models to be available in the States, following the Yanmar agreement, was the 950. The one shown has the optional MFWD and ROPS.

This 1630 is equipped with the new MFWD, supplied as an option by an outside supplier, and the OPU or Operator's Protection Unit, supplied in Europe as a very good interim safety cab until the new factory in Bruchsal could be brought on line with the SG2 Sound-Gard cab.

To round out the 40 series the 2840 became the 2940, with its engine displacement increased from 329 to 359 cubic inches. Being built in Mannheim, it had the MFWD option. At the top end of the scale the 8440 and 8640 replaced the 8430 and 8630, both showing a slight increase in horsepower when tested at Nebraska.

Enter The 1980s

The new decade started with the addition of a third Yanmar-built model, the 3-cylinder 33-horsepower 1050 fitted with a turbocharged version of the 950 engine. The smaller 14.5-horsepower 650 and 18.5-horsepower 750 followed in 1981 as models chiefly used in consumer product applications.

During the summer a new factory at Bruchsal, near Mannheim, came on line. It was designed chiefly as the parts center for Europe, but the new SG2 Sound-Gard cab was also made there. This meant that new tractor models from Mannheim, the 2040S, 4040S, and 4240S, were offered with this cab option; they also had increased power over the standard models.

Other models available with the new cab were the 1640 thru 3140, as well as European combines. Australia took the 1040, 1640, 2140, and 3140 from Germany, and from Argentina the 2140 and 3140.

The following year another new cab from Bruchsal was introduced, designed for tractors used in low buildings. It was similar in construction to the OPU, had built-in safety frame, and was an option on the smaller 40 series tractors.

When the 40 series tractors were updated in the States they were redesigned to take the SG2 cab mentioned in the previous photo. This 2040 has the alternative 4-post Roll-Gard ROPS.

Deere Tractors Worldwide—An Initial Survey

Giving a good impression of its size and power, the 8850 could cope with implements like this drawn chisel up to 59 feet wide. Due to the width of its 370-hp V-8 engine it had a hood wide enough to allow a six-lamp cluster of headlights.

In the States, 1982 saw the first Waterloo-built 50 series appear in the 4-wheel-drive models 8450, 8650, and the new V-8-engined 303.99-PTO-horsepower 8850, Deere's largest tractor to date.

Also added to the line in 1982 was a larger model from Yanmar, the 40-horsepower 1250. The 2940 in the States and the similar 3140 in Canada were offered with the Sound-Gard SG2 cab.

For the rest of the world, 1982 held other developments. By 1981 Chamberlain-John Deere had sold 50,000 tractors in Australia, and in 1982 Welshpool updated their models to the B series 3380B, 4080B, 4280B, and 4480B with small changes to the styling and specifications. The Mannheim-built 1640 thru 3140 were offered with MFWD and SG2 cabs. In Argentina the 4040 went into production for the following two years.

Deere acquired controlling interest in the South African operation in 1962 and formed John Deere (Pty) Ltd., with its factory at Nigel. A line of tillage implements and planting equipment was built, supplemented by tractors imported from Mannheim. The South African government decided that these must have some local input, and, following the establishment of Atlantis Diesel Engines (ADE), an offshoot of Perkins, it was decided these engines should be incorporated in the Mannheim units when sold in South Africa.

Development work was the result of combined Mannheim/Nigel cooperation, and in February 1982 production started on the new 41 series tractors, based on the European 40 series. Initially the news of this resulted in record sales of the imported 40 series of 3,076 units in 1981, but the performance of the new homemade line soon satisfied farmers of its reliability and it remained in production for the next five years.

The first models in the 41 series were the 4-cylinder 1641 standard, 1641F narrow and 2141, and the 6-cylinder 3141; two further turbocharged models, both 4-cylinder, the 2541 and 2941, were added two years later.

The 6-cylinder ADE-engined 3641 was available as shown with the new MFWD as an option, as was the two-post ROPS.

24

The U.S. 50 Series

Late in 1982 The Long Green Line became even longer with the announcement of the 50 series, the largest number of new tractors introduced at one time. All 10 models were available with Caster/Action mechanical front-wheel drive; the five largest were built in Waterloo and the five smaller in Mannheim. Dubuque became an exclusive industrial-equipment plant.

The late Lloyd Bellin discusses the merits of 4850-MFWD, Serial No. 13,514, with its driver, Alan Quamme, in Arizona in January 1990.

The 10 models were the 45-horsepower 2150, 55-horsepower 2350, 65-horsepower 2550, 75-horsepower 2750, and 85-horsepower 2950 from Europe and the 100-horsepower 4050, 120-horsepower 4250, 140-horsepower 4450, 165-horsepower 4650, and 190-horsepower 4850. Also available for specialist use were the 50-horsepower 2255 in vineyard or orchard form, the 2750 in either Low-Profile or Hi-Clearance (Mudder) guise, and the 4250 Hi-Crop. A new 15-speed Power Shift transmission was available for the five larger models, standard on the 4850.

Fuel efficiency was extremely important in the early 1980s with fuel costs rising to 35% of the tractor costs to the operator. The optional 4-wheel drive contributed to the reputation for economy which these new models soon acquired. Acceptance of this option was assured with the unique 13-degree Caster/Action tilt of the front wheels, which overcame the previous criticism of 4-wheel-drive tractors for their large turning radius.

When tested at Nebraska, the 4850 established itself as the most fuel efficient of all 2-wheel-drive tractors over 70 PTO horsepower in production at that time. It also pulled over 2,000 pounds more at the drawbar than any previous similar tractor. Another record was broken by the 4050 which achieved 70.0 dB(A) sound level at 50-percent engine speed in its Sound-Gard body.

With these developments in the States, Mexico tractor production was rationalized in 1983 with the introduction of two basic models, the 2755 and 4255, followed the next year with the 4455 Turbo (The 2755 and 4455 were still in production in Saltillo at the time of writing).

This photo gives an excellent impression of the extra height of the Hi-Crop models.

Deere Tractors Worldwide—An Initial Survey

Last of the Australian Line

In Australia the last tractor line to be produced in Welshpool was announced in 1985. This was the 90 series, available as both 2-wheel-drive models and with the 13-degree Caster/Action MFWD option. This one addition could add up to 20% to the drawbar pull.

The second Chamberlain color scheme of yellow with black trim was finally abandoned in favor of

The largest and last of the Chamberlain line of tractors as depicted on the final Australian-built-tractor brochure. The 4690-MFWD is pulling an Australian-built 300 series chisel plow or scarifier.

the Deere green and yellow, but retained the name Chamberlain on the otherwise similar decals and "television screen" trademark. The 94-horsepower 4090, 110-horsepower 4290, 129-horsepower 4490, and 154-horsepower 4690 all had 6-cylinder engines, the three larger were turbocharged, and all had a 12-speed-forward, 4-speed-reverse Hi-Lo transmission. Unlike previous series, all were offered with 3-point linkage option.

Their styling and equipment closely resembled the U.S. 50 series and included such items as multiple-stack hydraulic outlets (up to four), ISO couplers, extending bottom links, hydrostatic steering, power wet-disk brakes, and Personal-Posture armchair seats. All models had adjustable rear wheels and the linkage ones had adjustable front axles. In 1986 all tractor production ceased at Welshpool. The decision was made to import the American models.

Economy Models Match the Times

In 1984 the tractor purchasing farmer in Europe was in a very cost-conscious mood. As a result, Mannheim, still making the 40 series, introduced seven new models: three L-P with low-profile cab for working in low buildings, the 1640, 2040, and 2140; and four X-E or economy models, priced specifically at the Ford, Massey-Ferguson, International Harvester, and Case opposition, though still with the SG2 cab, models 1640, 2040, 2040S, and 2140. MFWD was also an option but other add-ons were kept to a minimum.

The Nebraska Test economy record holder when tested in November 1983, Test No. 1506, the 1650 was the largest model produced by Yanmar for Deere. This example was at the first EXPO on July 26, 1987.

Record-Breaking Yanmar Line

In Argentina the 4040 was replaced by the 4050 for a further two-year production, while on the home market two more and larger Yanmar models, the 50-horsepower 1450 and 60-horsepower 1650, completed that line. The latter was to make a name for itself by achieving the best-ever economy figures for any tractor tested at Nebraska. The three largest Yanmar-built models held nine records between them for fuel efficiency and lugging ability.

On the American market, although the larger Yanmar-built tractors overlapped in power with some of those from Mannheim, the former were sold as "lean and trim"

The 3640 was the largest 40 series model built in Mannheim. This photo illustrates the front hitch and PTO which became popular in Europe sometime before its acceptance in the States.

models and the German-built tractors as the deluxe machines.

In Mexico the decision was made to build a 60-horsepower model, and the result was the announcement of the 2755. These were to be built in the recently acquired former-International Harvester factory in Saltillo.

Mannheim's Largest Model Has MFWD As Standard

Mannheim announced its largest tractor yet, the 112-DIN-horsepower 3640 with MFWD as standard and an optional front 3-point hitch and PTO. This gave multi-implement capacity for the first time on a Deere tractor and brought a whole new concept to mechanized farming. With almost 50/50 front-to-rear weight ratio and its MFWD, the new 3640 was ideally equipped for this new type of operation.

China came back with a $25 million order for 400 tractors, 500 drills, 200 cultivators, and 100 European combines, and finally in 1984 the one millionth John Deere garden tractor was built.

The first John Deere tractor to have MFWD as standard equipment in the States arrived in 1985 with the introduction of the 95-horsepower 3150-MFWD. It was advertised as the first tractor to genuinely replace that all-time classic, the 4020. At the same time the 4050 engine was increased from 100 to 105 horsepower.

Deere Tractors Worldwide—An Initial Survey

Late in the year the 4350 with a 140-horsepower engine was announced in Europe for the 1986 season. It was in every aspect a Waterloo-design tractor though not appearing in the States. In Argentina the 3540 was announced to complete their 40 series line.

Specialist Models

A compact utility line of three tractors was announced, essentially for the grounds care products market. Shiftless hydrostatic transmissions and dual-pedal speed and direction control, leaving the hands free, distinguished them from previous models of the same size. They were the 16-horsepower 655, 20-horsepower 755, and 24-horsepower 855.

Another specialist tractor with a Yanmar-built engine was the 25-horsepower 900 HC. Reminiscent of the "L" and "LA" of the 1940s, it had a similar offset engine to give better visibility for row-crop work, but was built higher to span crops such as strawberries, tobacco, and other nursery and truck garden crops.

50 Series for Europe

Late in 1986 the complete Mannheim line changed to the 50 series, from the 38-horsepower 1350 to the 114-horsepower 3650 and the 140-horsepower 4350 already mentioned. From Waterloo the 4450, 4650, and 4850 were imported and given European lighting, hand brakes, etc.

Largest of the three compact utility models built chiefly for the grounds care products line, the 855 could find a niche on certain farms.

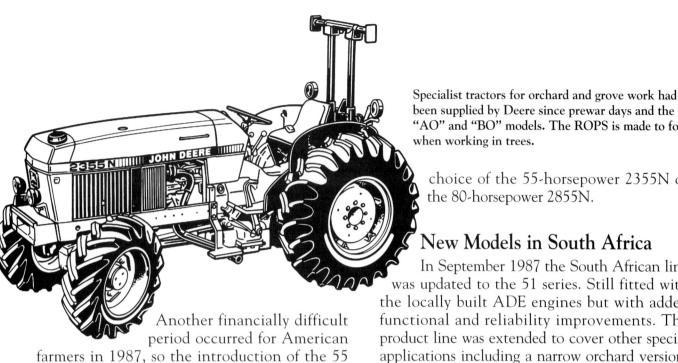

Specialist tractors for orchard and grove work had been supplied by Deere since prewar days and the "AO" and "BO" models. The ROPS is made to fold when working in trees.

Another financially difficult period occurred for American farmers in 1987, so the introduction of the 55 series of Mannheim-built 45- to 86-horsepower tractors with their 10 percent greater fuel economy was welcomed. The 3-cylinder 2155 and 4-cylinder 2355 and 2555, when equipped with collar-shift transmission, used a naturally aspirated engine. When the 2555 had the optional TSS transmission it used a turbocharged engine. The 2755 and 2955 were equipped with TSS as standard, but the 2955 also had additional Hi-Lo as standard.

Also available was a direction reverser for those tractors with a CS gearbox, permitting the operator to reverse direction without clutching. For use in vineyards and orchards there was a choice of the 55-horsepower 2355N or the 80-horsepower 2855N.

New Models in South Africa

In September 1987 the South African line was updated to the 51 series. Still fitted with the locally built ADE engines but with added functional and reliability improvements. The product line was extended to cover other special applications including a narrow orchard version, the 40-PTO-kW 2251N, and the Transtill 55-PTO-kW model 2651T, capable of 25-mph speed for those with long-distance transport problems of sugar cane and timber.

The smallest model was the derated 46-kW 2251. All models could have either TWD (2-wheel drive in South Africa) or MFWD except the largest 82-kW 3651, which was standard with MFWD. Only the 72-kW 2951 was turbocharged, but the 2351, 2651, 3351, and 3651 had altitude-compensated engines for use in high-altitude work on the Highveld. Only the two larger tractors had Roll-Gard ROPS as standard, it being optional on the smaller models.

The 2251N orchard model is fitted with a fully rated 52-kW ADE 236 NA engine and, as with the rest of the Nigel models except the largest, could be ordered with either 2-wheel drive (TWD in South Africa) or Caster/Action MFWD as shown here.

Deere Tractors Worldwide—An Initial Survey

A 3-cylinder turbocharged model, the 62-horsepower 1950, was added to the European line in 1988, while in Argentina three new models were announced: the 4-cylinder turbocharged 95-engine-horsepower 2850 and two 6-cylinder models, the naturally aspirated 110-horsepower 3350, and the turbocharged 125-horsepower 3550.

The 2850 was 2-wheel drive, the 3550 was 4-wheel drive, and the 3350 was available with either. The 4-wheel-drive tractors had the universal Caster/Action MFWD as in other areas. These models remained in production at the end of 1993.

Denver Announcement of Large 60 Series

Announced at a special meeting in Denver in the fall of 1988, it was the turn of the large articulated 4-wheel-drive models to be completely redesigned for 1989. The production of the V-8 engine at the Waterloo engine works had proved uneconomic, so the decision was made to use a 14-liter Cummins engine in the largest of the new 4-wheel-drive 60 series tractors. The 200-PTO-horsepower 8560 had a 235-horsepower 7.6-liter engine, the 256-PTO-horsepower 8760 a 300-horsepower 10.1-liter, and the largest 322-PTO-horsepower 8960 had the 370-horsepower 14-liter Cummins.

The Sound-Gard body for these tractors was changed to include a new side-access door and a one-piece upper windshield. This design, with the muffler and air intake moved to the right side of the cab, improved visibility. The tractors represented a totally new concept in this size of machine, with an all-new longer-wheelbase chassis with center frame oscillation.

The open-station tractors based on Mannheim models were the popular types for the Argentine market.

This triple-wheeled 8960 towers above the "giant" 8020 of the 1960s at the 1992 EXPO III in Waterloo, Iowa.

Deere's Largest-Ever Introduction

Palm Springs was host in January 1989 to the largest introduction of new Deere tractors and equipment to date. In addition to the new 60 series 4-wheel-drive models, the complete Waterloo line was updated to the 55 series. A sixth model was added, the 156-horsepower 4555, but it was not exported to Europe. All models had a redesigned 7.6-liter (466-cu. in.) engine. The 4955, Deere's first 200-horsepower row-crop model, set another fuel economy record when tested at Nebraska.

The three smaller models—4055, 4255, and 4455, had a narrower frame and were distinguishable by the four built-in headlamps, while the wider-framed 4555, 4755, and 4955 had five. Backed with a 5-year/5,000-hour warranty, the new series were designated Pacesetters with modified Sound-Gard bodies, new wheels designed to prevent tire wobble, and electronic sensing on the three-point hitch of the three larger models.

The 4255 Hi-Crop replaced the 4250-HC, the 2755 Hi-Clearance replaced the 2750 Mudder, and a new 6-cylinder 2955 Hi-Clearance model joined the line for the vegetable farmer.

The hydrostatic compact line of tractors had a fourth model added, the 33-engine-horsepower/27-PTO-horsepower 955. These were built in the newly opened Augusta factory in Georgia, which represented a change of thinking from the late 1970s when it was thought uneconomic to build under-40-horsepower tractors in the United States.

Meanwhile another series of five compact utility models was announced, the 70 series, ranging from the 18.5-engine/16-PTO-horsepower 670 to the 38.5-engine/35-PTO-horsepower 1070, and replacing the 650 thru 1050 models.

All models could have MFWD, ROPS was standard, and the two smaller had transmission-driven rear PTO, while the three larger had continuous live. The four smaller models had 3-cylinder engines, while the 1070 had a 4-cylinder.

With the introduction of the 55 series Waterloo tractors at Palm Springs an extra model was added to the line. The smallest of the larger models, the 156-hp 4555, is outside the Training Center at Davenport, Iowa, in both 2-wheel and MFWD format on August 9, 1990.

Largest of the compact utility 70 series, the 35-PTO-hp 1070 is equally at home on the farm or in the garden.

Deere Tractors Worldwide—An Initial Survey

A Goldoni-built 1745F at work cultivating in an orchard with its ROPS folded.

Spain Specializes

In Spain the decision was made in 1987 for Getafe to produce the specialist models, from the 46- to the 105-horsepower size, required in Europe. Getafe was also responsible for marketing other specialist models built by Goldoni in Italy.

Initially an arrangement was made with Goldoni to supply three orchard/vineyard tractors: the 42-horsepower 445, 49-horsepower 604, and 60-horsepower 614. These were soon replaced with four new models: the 42-horsepower 1445F, 48-horsepower 1745F, 56-horsepower 1845F, and 67-horsepower 2345F. These tractors were fitted with Saran-built engines and filled a specialist need on many of the smaller farms in southern Europe.

In addition there were seven smaller models from 21 to 42 engine horsepower: four with rigid frames, 933, 938, 1038, and 1042; and three with articulated, the 921, 933, and U238, which were compact 4-wheel-drive models with four equal-size wheels. There were also four small 2-wheel models from 8 to 18 horsepower.

The Spanish-built models were vineyard (V), orchard (F for fruteros), and Multi- or Hi-Crop (M). The addition of the letter A indicated 4WD. There were the 1750V, 1850V, 1850F and FA, 1950F and FA, 2450F and FA, 2650F and FA, 1850M, and 2450M. The standard 2-wheel-drive (S) and 4-wheel-drive (S-DT) models from the 1750 to the 3650 were imported from Mannheim. The 2450 and larger 2WD and MFWD standard tractors had the option of the SG2 cab and the front hitch and PTO combination.

A line up of new high-clearance tractors in the works grounds at Getafe on April 5, 1989. At least two 1850M and two 2450M are evident.

Posed for the front cover of their sales brochure, these two models represented the last Mannheim 6-cylinder tractors for the American market.

With a continuing depression in the States and with the advantage of hindsight, 1990 was not a year of change in the Deere tractor world. The only new model to appear was the replacement of the 3150-MFWD by the largest Taskmaster, the 3155-MFWD, still with a naturally aspirated engine. One significant event occurred, however, in Europe. The MC1 cab for tractors used in low buildings, which had been in service since 1986, was replaced with a new Console-Comfort cab or CC2. This unit had a clear deck and entrance through doors on both sides, a foretaste of things to come.

With the fitting of a turbocharged engine the 3155 became the 100-horsepower 3255 and was only available with MFWD. To fill the gap between it and the 85-horsepower 2955, the 92-horsepower 3055 was offered in 2-wheel-drive form only, and with the option of Roll-Gard ROPS or Sound-Gard body.

60 Series Row-Crop Tractors for 1991

The three larger Waterloo models were updated in 1991 with the air intake and muffler put under the hood and the exhaust extension moved to the right corner of the cab for a clear view ahead, as had already been achieved with the articulated series. The cab had easier access with corner steps; the batteries were beneath the top step. Caster/Action MFWD was optional on all three models.

One of the photos used in the 1994 Deere calendar was this contrast showing 30 years of tractor development: the 3020 of 1963 and the 4960-MFWD of 1993.

Deere Tractors Worldwide—An Initial Survey

The three 5000 series tractors outside the new works in Augusta, Georgia. The 5300 and 5200 2-wheel-drive models flank the 5400-MFWD.

5000 Series Announced

Late in 1991 an event occurred similar to that in 1959 with the introduction of an apparent out-of-sequence series called the 5000. Built in the new Augusta factory, there were three models from 40 to 60 horsepower: the 3-cylinder 5200, 5300, and 5400, the latter turbocharged, and all with MFWD option. The object behind their introduction was a quality tractor at an affordable price.

By moving the controls to a console on the right side and moving the whole station further forward and lower down, access from either side was easier. A folding rollover protective structure (ROPS) and the option of horizontal exhaust ensured a low-profile tractor for work in orchards or old low buildings.

Servicing was made easy with a tilt-up hood and side panels removable without tools. The fuel tank was now rear mounted to avoid the danger of spills in the engine area or operator's station.

A 9-speed-forward, 3-reverse simple collar-shift transmission with first and reverse opposite each other for quick change of direction and with differential lock ensured maximum flexibility and performance. Tandem-pump hydraulic design gave adequate power for steering and brakes, plus a large reserve for implement control.

A "New" New Generation

The year 1992 saw a breakthrough in design and performance of tractors by the company's engineers equivalent to the New Generation of 1960. The result of an investment of several hundred million dollars, the new 6000 and 7000 series represented a complete change from existing tractors, so complete in fact that only nine parts were carried over from the existing line.

The reason that only the three larger Waterloo models were upgraded in 1991 became apparent in 1992 with the announcement of the completely new 6-cylinder 7000 series from Waterloo. At the same time Mannheim announced the equally revolutionary 4-cylinder 6000 series.

The extra grip of 4-wheel drive is not required by this 7700, hard at work with forage harvester and forage wagon in tow.

The U.S. models consist of the 110-horsepower 7600, 125-horsepower 7700, and 140-horsepower 7800. They have an all-new modular design encompassed in a 12-mm-thick independent steel frame. This allows a significant reduction in the overall weight of the tractor. Everything about the 7000 series is new—engine, transmission, hydraulics, cab, latest Caster/Action MFWD, modular-design PTO, and electrohydraulic hitch.

The new ComfortGard cab, with its 72 dB(A) sound level is the quietest tractor cab in the world. With doors on both sides, 40 percent more space than the one it replaced, and much more glass area (29%), it answers all the requests made by users and dealers alike.

The seat now has air-cushioned suspension with 4-way attenuation, and perhaps most revolutionary of all, the instrument panel or command column tilts with the steering wheel to provide a constant viewpoint for the operator. There is also a completely new system for uniform air distribution. Altogether, a cab that suits the severest critic.

Not overlooked is the position of the external lights, with two corner forward lights at low level, adjustable beltline lamps, and eight cab roof lights for overall lighting—14 powerful halogen lights in all.

Again the 6.8-liter (7600) and 7.6-liter (7700 and 7800) engines are completely new, with engine rpm governed to 2,100. With poly-vee fan belt, 140-amp alternator, state-of-the-art turbochargers, vertical oil filter for spill prevention, and tailor-made fuel injection equipment, the new engines are truly designed for the future.

A large European dealer meeting was called in Germany to announce a completely new European combine line, the Z 2000 series. Also introduced was the new 4-cylinder 6000 series tractors to be built in Mannheim, filling the gap between the Waterloo 6-cylinder series and the 3-cylinder 5000 series from Augusta.

Four models were announced for Europe: the 75-engine-horsepower 6100, 84-engine-horsepower 6200, 90-engine-horsepower 6300, and 100-engine-horsepower 6400. The last three are turbocharged and are available in the States; the 6100, however, is not offered in the United States.

An inside view of the deluxe conditions prevailing in the new ComfortGard cabs fitted to the 6000 and 7000 tractors.

This cross section of the 7800 reveals the very different design features of the new models compared with those they replaced.

35

Deere Tractors Worldwide—An Initial Survey

The design of the 4-cylinder series closely follows the 6-cylinder 7000 series. The new full-frame design was adopted with engines moved forward to increase front weight with the now increasingly popular MFWD and front hitch. Transmissions on the 6000 series are the SynchroPlus for the less intensive user with the choice of 12 speeds forward, 4 reverse or 15/5 or 18/6, plus an optional 9 forward/ 3 reverse creeper range available.

The alternative is the PowrQuad as on the 7000 series, with the choice of 16/12, 20/16, or 24/16 versions for the 6000 series, the latter two in Europe only, or 20/12 on the 7000. Its optional transmission is the Power Shift with 19 forward, 7 reverse.

In Europe the ComfortGard cab is called the TechCenter cab, and is the same design for all seven models, giving 72 dB(A) on the 6-cylinder models, 75 dB(A) sound level on the 4-cylinder.

On the smaller series the complete cab can be tilted sideways, after removing the right wheel, giving easy access to the transmission for repair or addition of more units. All the systems remain connected—steering and brakes, hydraulics, air conditioner, heater, gear-shifting, SCV controls, and wiring harness. Many other repair jobs can be done without tilting, through access hatches in the cab floor.

The advantages of the optional front PTO and hitch are apparent in this photo of a 6400 mowing and conditioning a wide swath.

A new line of front loaders matching the new tractors was introduced at the same time: the 540A for 3- and 4-cylinder tractors up to 70 horsepower, the 640A for the new 6000 series, and the 740A for 6-cylinder models. Attachments for manure loading, pallet lifting, silage cutting, and grain, bale, and material handling are only some of those available.

Standard equipment includes the Quick-Park parking stands and mid-mount couplers, with no tools required to attach or detach. The new tractors can be ordered with optional single-lever control for the above; with the older series tractors it was ordered with the loader.

Another occasion when MFWD was not required is illustrated with this 6300 cultivating corn.

36

A Fourth Model in Updated 70 Series Four-Wheel-Drive Tractors

The three 4-wheel-drive models of the 60 series became four when the new POWER-PLUS 70 series was announced for 1993. Power has been increased from 235 horsepower on the 7.6-liter-engined 8560 to 250 horsepower on the 8570, and remains at 300 horsepower on the new 10.1-liter engine of the 8770. It reaches 350 horsepower on the new 8870 fitted with the 10.1-liter engine, and 400 horsepower for the first time in a Deere tractor with the 14-liter-engined 8970.

The three larger models can now be fitted with triple tire options with cast drive wheels and steel duals, giving increased flotation and reduced soil compaction. With almost 15,000-pound lift capacity on their three-point hitch and adjustable wheel spacings, the new models are well suited to work in narrow row spacings.

Factory- or field-installed 1,000-rpm PTO option is available on all four models, irrespective of the type of transmission fitted. A 12-speed Syncro is standard on all models, 24-speed Powr-Sync is optional on all four, and a 12-speed Power Shift can be ordered on the three larger.

Two other innovations should be mentioned: 1) An exclusive Electronic Engine Control allows the 8870, for example, to develop an extra 25 horsepower, or 375 engine horsepower total, when pulling through tough spots. There are similar increases for the other models. 2) Field Cruise Control allows the operator to set the engine rpm at whatever speed he wishes for constant pace in performing seeding, planting, chemical application, and any other job requiring speed accuracy. A foot-operated decelerator switch allows speed reduction while turning, before automatically resuming the required operating speed.

Massive grip and pulling power is illustrated by this triple-tired 8870 disking a Western field.

Deere Tractors Worldwide—An Initial Survey

6000 and 7000 Series Extended

The missing models in the 100-horsepower range were introduced in the fall of 1993. Two completely new 6-cylinder turbocharged models were announced from Waterloo: the 92-PTO-horsepower 7200 and the 100-PTO-horsepower 7400 joined the three larger 110- to 145-PTO-horsepower 7000 series models.

Available as 2- or 4-wheel-drive tractors, the new models can also be purchased in either Hi-Crop or High-Clearance (Mudder) mode. In addition to the models fitted with the ComfortGard cab, open-station tractors are now offered to customers in markets not requiring the protection of a cab. A standard feature is a foldable two-post ROPS for use in restricted spaces. Many of the features of the models with cabs including right-side console, flat platform, and fully adjustable seat and steering column are also standard equipment.

From Mannheim the 6-cylinder turbocharged 6000

A light job in a hayfield for a 7400-MFWD with round baler on a pleasant summer's day. The introduction of the 6000 and 7000 series saw different models in the 100-plus-hp range for Europe and the States—the 6600 and 6800 from Mannheim, the 7200 and 7400 from Waterloo.

series models appeared some 12 months after their 4-cylinder counterparts. The 110-engine-horsepower 6600 has a 6T/5880 Saran-built engine and the top-of-the-line 6800 has a 6T/6786 engine. The bore on all 6000 series tractors is the same, 106.5 millimeters, but the stroke is 127 millimeters on the 6100, 6400, and 6800, and 110 millimeters on the 6200, 6300, and 6600. Rated speed is 2,300 rpm on all but the 6800 which is 2,100 rpm.

The three smaller models use Category 2 linkage, while the three larger use Category 2/3N. New SCV couplers can be connected or disconnected under pressure. A front hitch and 1,000-rpm PTO with either 6- or 21-spline shaft are optional equipment on all models. The 6800's rear PTO is shiftable 540E/1,000 only. The rest of the series has a shiftable 540/540E/1,000 option and the 4-cylinder tractors can have a 540-rpm PTO.

A new 120-hp 6800-MFWD complete with front PTO and hitch makes its way homeward with folded disks in tow.

Around the World In '93

At the Getafe factory in Spain the specialist orchard, vineyard, and high-crop models continue to be the 3- and 4-cylinder 50 series through to the end of 1993 and for some months to come.

The only new models introduced are two larger 4-wheel-drive articulated tractors from Goldoni with equal-size wheels, the EURO 42 and EURO 50, both available in two forms depending on wheel size. The 42AW and 50A have either 18- or 15.3-inch wheels; the 42BW and 50B have 16-inch.

Both models have 3-cylinder engines, the EURO 42 of 37 horsepower and the EURO 50 42 horsepower. Category 1 or 1N linkage was optional on both. Styling is similar to the earlier models and the rollbar is of the folding type now used on all the small orchard and vineyard tractors. They represent a useful additional source of power for the many small fruit farmers in the world.

First country to introduce the new Zetor 2000 series is Mexico with the 74-hp 2300, largest of the naturally aspirated 4-cylinder models, illustrated here in open-station format with ROPS.

At the time of this writing, Mexico continues to build the various 2755 models which have been in production since 1984, together with the 4455. The 2000 series from Zetor are planned to be introduced and assembled there in 1994.

Economy Models from Czech Republic

Late in 1993 Hans Becherer, company chairman, announced an agreement with Zetor, the Czech Republic tractor manufacturer, to market eight of their models as a low-price line for emerging markets, particularly in Asia, Australia, and Central and South America.

The line consists of one 3-cylinder 49-horsepower Model 2000, four 4-cylinder tractors, the naturally aspirated 2100 with 62 engine horsepower, 2200 with 68 horsepower, and 2300 with 74 horsepower, and the turbocharged 2400 with 81 horsepower. Three larger 4-cylinder models top the line, all turbocharged—the 89-horsepower

Latest of the articulated models from Goldoni, the EURO 50 is the largest of this type of tractor with a 3-cylinder 42-hp engine.

Deere Tractors Worldwide—An Initial Survey

Lowest powered of the three new larger-type Czech-built tractors, the 75-PTO-hp 2700 is otherwise similar in appearance to the 86-PTO-hp 2800 and the most powerful model, the 91-PTO-hp 2900 (see chapter 8).

2700, 100-horsepower 2800, and 106-horsepower 2900. PTO horsepower is, respectively, 43, 54, 60, 66, 72, 75, 86, and 91.

All eight models can be purchased with cab or rollbar and with 2WD or MFWD. The three largest tractors have 8-forward-speed, 8-reverse synchronized transmissions with reverser as standard, optional 16F/4R with power Hi/Lo. The five smaller have 10-forward, 2-reverse speeds with optional 10F/10R with reverser. Hydrostatic steering is standard on all models; hydraulically operated disk brakes are used on the five smaller, wet-disk hydraulically operated on the three larger.

It had been decided to use the new arrangement with the Czech Republic and import the 2000, 2300, and 2800 Zetor-built models for the Argentinian market during 1994.

Equipped with MFWD and open station or a modern-looking cab, the new tractors blend in well with the rest of the John Deere line when painted in the familiar green and yellow.

By the end of 1993 the future of the South African operation was in the melting pot, awaiting the outcome of the country's pending elections. The 51 series, which had been in production since 1987, was reduced to three basic tractors: the 2251, 2351, and 2651.

Production of the 4-cylinder turbocharged 2951 and 6-cylinder 3351 and 3651 had ceased and the last of the 3350 and 3650 models built in Mannheim were imported as an interim measure.

With the Australasian market supplied by Mannheim, Waterloo, and probably some of the Zetor models, tractors bearing the company's name and supplied to world markets have changed considerably over the last eight years, both in where they are built and in which country's factories.

The result of an agreement with the French Renault concern would mean still further involvement with other tractor builders, started back in 1956 with the purchase of Lanz in Germany, followed by that of Chamberlain in Australia, the Japanese models from Yanmar, the specialist Goldoni models from Italy, and now the 2000 series from Zetor and the Czech Republic.

The next 100 years will doubtless be as interesting as the past have been . . .

Smallest of the three surviving models built in Nigel, the 2251 is fitted with a derated 4-cylinder 46-kW ADE 236 naturally aspirated engine.

40

Product Review

The 2-Cylinder Era, Part 1: 1893-1951

From the single-cylinder Froelich and various 2-cylinder Waterloo Boy models to the long line of John Deere's own 2-cylinder tractors, starting with the 15-27 Model "D" in 1923 to the 65-horsepower 830 diesel of 1959, we explore the development of one of the world's most popular and simple tractor designs.

The First 30 Years

Following the introduction of the world's first successful tractor, the Froelich, the interest in the "mechanical horse" gradually grew in the farming community and its implement suppliers. Several John Deere branches expressed a wish to have a tractor to sell, and at least one took on the agency for the Big Four gas tractor built in Minneapolis. The Big Four 30 was a slightly smaller version of the 45 shown.

This encouraged Deere to experiment with it own designs, starting in 1912 and culminating in the production of 100 All-Wheel-Drive models in 1918—the first tractor to carry the John Deere name. The purchase of the Waterloo Gasoline Engine Company on March 18 of that year ensured, however, that Deere would follow the 2-cylinder idea for more than the next 40 years.

The single-cylinder Froelich and other experimental models of the nineteenth century gave way at the Waterloo factory to large 4-cylinder cross-mounted machines and 2-cylinder horizontally opposed models. This was before the pattern was finally set in 1914 with the horizontal 2-cylinder 4-stroke Model "R," capable of burning kerosene and other low-cost fuels.

Marketed by some branch houses, the Big Four tractors were available in two models, the 30 and 45. This EB45 is owned by Harold Ottoway of Grail, Kansas, and is now located permanently at the Divide County Museum, Crosby, North Dakota. John Tysse, caught in the background, gives an idea of the size of these tractors.

One of the two known surviving All-Wheel-Drive models of the 100 built in 1918. This tractor, No. 79, owned by Frank Hansen of Rollingstone, Minnesota, is the most original, and can be seen at many of the annual vintage shows around the States. Here it was exhibited at the Northern Farm Show in Minneapolis in 1992.

Five tractors lined up after they were first built.

An early example of the Model "R" single-speed Waterloo Boy, style E, Serial No. 1,643, owned by Ken Kass and seen at the first Two-Cylinder Club EXPO in 1987. Once believed to be used on Overtime models, the vertical fuel tank was in fact an option on early models.

Mr. Leavitt's 1913 half-track conversion of the Waterloo Boy 25-hp Standard model is shown. New evidence has appeared recently that one of these tractors was used prewar in North Dakota. This page was taken from a Waterloo Boy Spreader brochure.

43

The 2-Cylinder Era, Part 1: 1893-1951

A letter to *The Green Magazine* by Leland E. Seth of South Dakota remembering seeing a Waterloo Boy "Sure Grip Never Slip" tractor plowing for tree planting in prewar North Dakota has confirmed that at least one of these tractors reached a farm.

Some 12 varieties of the Waterloo Boy Model "R" were produced between 1914 and 1918. Over 8,000 tractors were built, nearly half going to the British Isles, where they were marketed as the Overtime tractor to help in the growing of food to support the World War I effort. In 1917 the Model "N" with two forward speeds was announced, and both the last series "R" and the "N" were in production when Deere took over the factory. A number of 2-speed models also carried the Overtime name.

Enter the "D"

Experiments had already been started by Waterloo, before the Deere purchase, to produce a tractor with internal final gear drives, and these continued under the new regime. The end result was the 1923 announcement of the famous Model "D."

Initially available with a 26-inch spoke flywheel and direct left-side steering, this was modified after 879 units had been built to a 24-inch spoke flywheel, thicker to give the same weight, with a jointed steering rod giving better clearance between it and the flywheel.

The oldest known example of an Overtime tractor is shown at Lackham Agricultural College Museum in Wiltshire, England. It is unique in having two serial numbers stamped on its crankshaft, 1,728 and 1,747. This fact is confirmed in the archive records—under entry for 1,728 it says "see 1,747."

An early chain-steer Model "N," Serial No. 14,420, owned by Derek and Janet Mellor of Peakdale, Derbyshire. Although an original Overtime, the tractor has been restored in Waterloo colors

Another example of five new tractors lined up for sale, these Overtimes were outside the premises of Frank Standen during World War I; he later became the first concessionaire for John Deere in England in 1935.

Making a nice comparison with Serial No. 14,420, this late Model "N," Serial No. 28,629, was found by the author in Canada and has been beautifully restored by its new owner, Brian Davey, of Thelnetham in England's East Anglia.

One of the various experimental Waterloo Boy "Pre 'D's" showing the typical engine layout, now reversed with its head to the front of the tractor, but still with the same style front and rear wheels.

The 2-Cylinder Era, Part 1: 1893-1951

The star exhibit at EXPO III was the 3/8-scale model shown opposite. The owner, Dennis Franz of Newton, Kansas, made it, having first dismantled an original tractor, measuring and reducing each component part. He began in 1990 and completed it after 2,500 hours in 1991.

Franz built the spark plugs, magneto, carburetor, governor, oil pump, priming cups, grease cups, and all gears (heat treated) by hand. The only castings were the flywheel, transmission, quills, radiator cap, fuel cap, and front hub caps. Lettering was cut out of brass with a jeweler's saw and soldered on.

The following were fabricated out of steel: crankcase, transmission case, front and rear axles, water cooled cylinders with cast iron liners, water cooled cylinder head with cast iron valve seats, seat, steering wheel, etc.

Pistons were made from solid bar stock. Crankshaft was fabricated out of seven pieces of steel, then ground and balanced.

Specifications: Weight 245 pounds, stroke 3 inches, bore 2 7/16 inches, full pressure oiling, approximately 1.5 horsepower, 400-900 rpm, height 21 inches, length excluding seat 41 inches, width 23 inches.

"Herbie," radio controlled, was added in 1992. He was completed in about 80 weeks and is controlled by a 6-channel radio and operated by eight electric motors and five micro switches.

Greeting everyone who visits the Dufners in Buxton, N. Dak., this assembly of 2-cylinder tractor parts also acts as a call to meals or the phone . .

A rare sight, three "Spoke D"s at the Layher's farm in Nebraska. On the left, Serial No. 30,432 purchased new by Lester's father in 1923; in the center, the tenth "D" built, Serial No. 30,410, both of these with ladder-type radiator sides and fabricated front axles; on the right, Serial No. 30,754 with the later front axle.

Another photo of Spoke "D," Serial No. 30,432, showing the radiator's ladder sides and original-style rear-wheel lugs.

46

The author's pride and joy, 24-in. spoke "D," Serial No. 34,628, at its first rally in August 1988 after completion of its restoration by Mick Ockwell of Blunsdon, near Swindon, Wiltshire. Ockwell is a well-known maker of tinwork for most makes and models of vintage tractors. This photo makes an interesting comparison with Serial No. 30,432.

Seen first by the author at the Midwest Old Threshers show at Mt. Pleasant, Iowa, in 1991 where this photo of Dennis Franz's 3/8-scale Model Spoke "D" was taken, before "Herbie" was added.

A work of art and the star of many vintage shows, the 3/8-scale Model "D" was built by Dennis Franz of Newton, Kansas. It is radio controlled at some distance giving the impression that "Herbie" is really in control.

The 2-Cylinder Era, Part 1: 1893-1951

D Variations

To return to rather larger machinery, in 1926 the keyed flywheel on the "D" was changed to the solid type. This, with the single keyway changed to 6-spline, remained a feature of the 2-cylinder tractors to the end.

Model "D"s were offered in various guises over the years. An orchard model, a change to three forward speeds, an industrial model, and even experimental crawler versions saw the light of day, but these latter were soon withdrawn. The model had its final update in 1939 when it received Dreyfuss styling to bring it in line with other models.

Model "D"s were exported all over the world, including a batch for Russia in the 1920s. The author was very pleased to obtain a new "D" on steel, Serial No. 154,757, in England on February 8, 1943, allocated to him as a custom operator by the war agricultural committee, for the sum of £415.

In spring 1943, the author is plowing a reasonably straight furrow with his new "D," Serial No. 154,757, in a 63-acre field near his home. The tractor was delivered February 8, 1943, for £415 ($1,660) on steel.

A very rough Model "D," Serial No. 68,803, with engine stuck and in need of extensive repairs, purchased by the author at a sale in a snowstorm!

The same tractor after its loving restoration by Derek Mellor of Peakdale, near Buxton, Derbyshire, in the heart of England.

This 2-speed "D," Serial No. 110,570, is not over extended with its 4B 2-bottom plow at a vintage plowing demonstration. The owner, James Coward of Thorney, Cambs., is at the wheel.

"DI," Serial No. 127,198, the property of the Layhers of Wood Green, Nebraska. Note the special seat on these tractors, which necessitated an extended offset clutch lever and throttle control.

An original Model "D," Serial No. 154,263, seen at the Divide County Museum, Crosby, North Dakota. This tractor, owned by John Tysse, is identical to the authors first new John Deere with exterior rims added.

The 2-Cylinder Era, Part 1: 1893-1951

A Smaller Row-Crop Tractor

Following the success of the "D" it was inevitable that farmers would ask for a smaller tractor and one capable of row-crop work like the competition's Farmall. The result was the Model "C" announced in 1927, and was soon altered to become the "GP." This 20-horsepower tractor was designed for 3-row work and adopted the 4-wheel configuration as a result. It was the first tractor supplying power in four ways—drawbar, PTO, belt, and mechanical lift.

Layhers' Model "C" on the display floor of the new Two-Cylinder Club's headquarters at Grundy Center, Iowa. This photo, taken by Jack Cherry editor of the Club's magazine, shows the unique features of the "C," wooden steering wheel, vertical seat support, level-across rear-wheel hubs and straight-cut exhaust end.

Don Huber is the proud owner of this Model "C," which is complete with water feed to the carburetor and its fourth power outlet, a mechanical lift.

One of the two "GP" Tricycle tractors known to have survived at the time of writing as found in Arizona by the Goulds of Pierson, Michigan. It was shown "as is" at EXPO II in 1990.

Thirty years production of the Model "D" is represented in this photo taken in the grounds of Deere's headquarters. On the left the Spoke "D" of 1923, center a "DI" from the late 1930s, and right a 1953 "D" Streeter, Serial No. 191,654, one of the last built.

The same "GP" Tricycle tractor after restoration at EXPO III in 1992.

51

The 2-Cylinder Era, Part 1: 1893-1951

A 2-Row Alternate

In the Southern states there was a requirement for a 2-row tractor with tricycle format. As a result the original "C" and tricycle "GP"s were updated to produce another and separately numbered series called the "GP" wide tread or "GPWT." A further development from this model was a tractor sold to the potato growers in Maine with narrower quills allowing its use in 38-inch rows. The resulting 203 units were called the Model "P" and again carried a different serial number series.

An early "GP," Serial No. 204,844, with air cleaner behind the original small-type radiator and stub exhaust, seen at the first EXPO in Waterloo, Iowa.

A 1929 "GP," Serial No. 211,806, with right-side vertical airstack but early stub exhaust. This "GP" is owned and restored by James Coward of Thorney near Peterborough, England.

The last styled "GP" with larger 6- × 6-in. engine, right-side exhaust and left-side bail-type air cleaner. Serial No. 228,305 was restored by Murray Simpson, Deere dealer in Fife, Scotland, and has now been sent to the Mannheim Works Museum. Note the differences in this 1931 tractor compared to the previous photo.

A very early side-steer "GPWT," Serial No. 400,047, outside the Layhers' home in Wood River, Nebraska. Note the air cleaner between the radiator and engine and the water connection to the carburetor as in all Model "D"s.

The Coblers from Ottumwa, Iowa, own this Model "P," Serial No. 5,164, with mid-mounted cultivator shown at the last two EXPOs.

The 2-Cylinder Era, Part 1: 1893-1951

Deere's First Orchard Model

One more customer requirement was satisfied when the standard "GP" was lowered to meet the needs of orchard farmers and called the "GPO." The first six were converted from wide treads and featured the crossover air intake fitted originally when the engine bore was increased to 6 inches. To retain a low profile on the "GPO," the air intake was extended above the initial stub exhaust alongside the hood and rear right fender.

A few of these orchard models were fitted with crawler tracks by Lindeman in Yakima, Washington, for use in the hilly orchard grounds of that state, and are now known as "GPO-Lindeman."

The final and most extensive visible modifications to the "GPWT" were adopted in 1932 when it received overhead steering in place of the side steer, allowing a much improved operator position. At the same time the hood was narrowed with a rearward taper and deepened to give the operator a better view of his work; muffler and air intake were brought within the hood width, adding to this effect.

With only 445 of this type built before the next major step occurred, these models are eagerly sought after by today's collectors.

From the very extensive Keller collection, this early "GPO," Serial No. 15,023, has the cross-over aircleaner pipe and is seen at EXPO III.

The opposite side shows the extended air cleaner intake pipe, Bruce Keller in attendance.

This "GPO," Serial No. 15,323, was seen at EXPO I with full citrus fenders and solid orchard-type front wheels. In the background another "GPO" can be seen, both tractors having the production-type muffler and bail air intake.

With their Swedish visitor, Johannes Calamnius, at the controls, the Layhers' "GPO," Serial No. 15,704, shows a variation in its air intake position from John Nikodyn's Serial No. 15,703 shown in *John Deere Tractors and Equipment Vol. 1*, page 126.

Overhead-steer "GPWT," Serial No. 404,405, complete with mechanical lift and on steel wheels. The rear wheels have protective rear rubber bands for show conditions. This tractor is owned by the Cobler family, Ottumwa, Iowa.

55

The 2-Cylinder Era, Part 1: 1893-1951

Hydraulics Replace Mechanical Lift

During 1933 another far-reaching step was taken with the introduction of a new row-crop tractor, the Model "A," with hydraulics replacing the mechanical lift of the "GP." It was preceded by several experimental tractors, some equipped with 4-speed transmissions, some with three speeds, the AA1 and AA3, respectively.

These 25-horsepower tractors were followed a year later by the 16-horsepower "B," and both were available in standard form with twin front wheels; later they could have either single front wheel ("AN" and "BN") or wide adjustable front axle ("AW" and "BW"). For certain crops a very narrow model, the "BW-40," was added and for crops requiring high clearance the "AWH" and "BWH" implemented the lengthening line.

This Model "AA" tractor with 2-furrow No. 4 plow was at work on October 2, 1933. Note the bail air cleaner as on the last GPWT. The tractor had no PTO and no lettering on the back axle.

A unique photo which came the author's way of three unstyled "A"s with single control on the front unit, plowing with an 8-bottom John Deere drawn plow.

An open-fanshaft "A," Serial No. 413,981, with flat spoke rears. Note the straight edge to the fillet below the frame.

Seen at a sale at Sigourney, Iowa, on August 1, 1987, this unstyled "AN," Serial No. 435,122, with rubber front made $1,900 while its spare front steel wheel made $1,050.

Consecutive numbered unstyled "AN," Serial No. 429,727, and "AW," Serial No. 429,728, at EXPO I.

This "AWH," Serial No. 472,018, is equipped with 40-in. rear French and Hecht spoke wheels at the first EXPO in Waterloo.

The 2-Cylinder Era, Part 1: 1893-1951

❶ Another photo of the Kellers' first unstyled production "B," Serial No. 1,000. The first 42,174 tractors had a short frame, but this was lengthened from Serial No. 42,200 to allow interchange of mid-mounted equipment with the "A"s.

❷ In very original condition, this short-frame "B," Serial No. 23,729, with underslung toolbar and rear ridgers is shown just as it was imported in 1936 to England by F.A. Standen & Sons of St. Ives, Huntingdon. It was seen at the Stradsett show on May 16, 1993.

❸ "BN," Serial No. 1,791, with experimental front wheel at EXPO I.

❹ A good view of the narrow front axle and rear wheel setting of this short-frame "BW-40" shown at EXPO III.

❺ Compare the height of the front spindles with the "BW." This "BWH," Serial No. 57,718, is another of the Keller collection from Kaukauna, Wisconsin.

❻ This side view emphasizes the long frame on this "BNH," Serial No. 46,175.

❼ The unstyled "BW" is more unusual; this example seen at EXPO II has the long frame and is on steel wheels with optional fenders.

❽ Compare this long-frame "B" on tip-toe steel wheels, Serial No. 55,181 with Serial No. 23,729. There are still signs of its original decals. It was at the Peterborough Vintage Club's annual get-together hosted by its owner, James Coward of Thorney.

59

The 2-Cylinder Era, Part 1: 1893-1951

Standard and Orchard Models Added

The introduction of the two new row-crop models meant that replacements for the "GP" standard tread and "GPO" orchard tractors were the next customer requirement. Accordingly in 1935 the "AR," "AO," "BR," and "BO" were announced to meet this demand.

It was one of the first of these, an "AR," Serial No. 259,256, which was supplied to the farm where the author worked in the spring of 1940, which can be blamed for his catching the "green and yellow bug" which has infected his thinking for the last 53 years. If the Allis-Chalmers WF ordered by the farmer had been delivered on time, his blood might have been orange!

Built September 20, 1935, this "AR," Serial No. 251,363, had an interesting life. It was built as an "AO" and was shown at the Waterloo Cattle Congress September 24, as the new orchard tractor. Afterwards it returned to the factory and later reappeared in Minnesota on October 15 as an "AR." It is currently owned by Tom Langan of La Crescent, Minnesota, who is its second owner.

The only photo the author could find of a pre-streamlined "AO," Serial No. 251,873, on steel wheels with full citrus fenders.

The apple of this author's eye.. An early "AR," Serial No. 256,743, on rubber, similar to the one delivered to Gloucestershire in 1940, photographed after removal from the container in Suffolk on January 4, 1992. Behind, the "BR" with round spokes had arrived in the same consignment.

Showing the unique dipstick on this tractor.

One of the two known remaining experimental "AOS" tractors, Serial No. 1,498, was originally No. 106. They have a unique oil dipstick in place of the usual level plug. This tractor is another in the extensive collection owned by Walter and Bruce Keller of Kaukauna, Wisconsin.

This "AI," Serial No. 252,334, forms part of the large Layher collection and is fitted with an original factory-built cab with access from the rear. The tractor also has electric lighting.

The second version of the "AR," Serial No. 260,409, with center radiator cap and larger 5.5- × 6.75-in. engine is the property of Julian Dimelow of Malpas, Cheshire, and is pictured at their local Malpas show.

61

The 2-Cylinder Era, Part 1: 1893-1951

Unlike the "AR" and "AO," the "BR" and "BO" were never styled. Smaller than the AR and AO, they were originally equipped with a 4.25- × 5.25-inch engine without compression taps. When the larger 4.5- × 5.5-inch engine from Serial No. 329,000 was fitted, taps became a necessity. Late models were often equipped with electric lighting and starting.

Lindeman Fills Crawler Niche

Following the unsuccessful experiment with a Model "D" on tracks, but after greater success with the "GPO," the Lindemans decided to use the "BO" as their base unit, and many hundreds of these were supplied to Western farmers and orchard growers.

As with the Model "DI," a few "AI" and "BI" were built for a short time, and because of their scarcity, are much sought after by collectors. The "BR" and "BO" were never styled, being replaced before new styling was applied to the standard and orchard models.

A photo sent by a Two-Cylinder Club member from Holland. This later version of the unstyled "AR" has electric starting and lighting and is seen at a show in that country. Note the special light brackets.

A nicely restored early "BR," Serial No. 325,677, has a small engine without compression taps and factory round-spoke wheels.

An "AO" at EXPO with similar lights, electric starting, and full citrus fenders. It has a semi-integral PTO-driven mower with hydraulic lift attached.

Part of Robert Dufel's beautiful collection of tractors at Hudson, Iowa (mostly on rubber, unusual for the United States), this "BO" has the optional full citrus fenders.

EXPO II saw this collection of three "BO"-Lindeman tractors with different variations pictured on July 23, 1990. The tractor nearest the camera has rubber padded track shoes; the center model is equipped with hydraulics to control its dozer blade, and has the downward fixed muffler; the outer two have radiator shutters.

The third industrial model in the Layhers' collection is this "BI," Serial No. 326,025, on 28-in. rears and spoke fronts, pictured in front of Lester's farmhouse. Note the seat fitted to industrial models and the strengthened front frame for mounting front attachments.

One of the last "BR"s built with electric starting and lighting and equipped with the later type 26-in. rear tires.

63

The 2-Cylinder Era, Part 1: 1893-1951

Dreyfuss Adds Styling

Although the company had streamlined the "AO" to protect branches in orchard work in 1936, it was in 1938 when the decision was made to employ Henry Dreyfuss to style not only their tractors, but also combines and other machines in the line.

The first fruits of this decision were the appearance in that year of the Models "A" and "B" with a new modern look, enclosing the steering mechanism and adding style to the overall appearance of the tractors but retaining the basic mechanical design.

Six Speeds Replace Four

The next change for the 1941 season was the addition of two further forward speeds to the row-crop models when equipped with rubber tires. Many tractors were supplied on steel wheels during the war, due to shortage of rubber, and in this case the two higher-speed gears were not fitted; many owners had these added as soon as conditions allowed.

This early 6-speed styled "A" has electric starting and lighting, necessitating an extended hood to house the battery, and Powr-Tool. The muffler should be the same height as the air stack.

Layhers' styled 4-speed "BWH"-40 makes an unusual and interesting exhibit at EXPO III.

This 6-speed "AN" was plowing at the World Plowing Match on September 19, 1984.

Right side view of 6-speed "AW," Serial No. 531,093, a tractor imported to England under the Lend-Lease wartime scheme, shown on the Cotswolds near Lechlade on November 7, 1984.

Seen at the Stradsett, Norfolk, vintage show, 6-speed "BN," Serial No. 121,892, is attached to a nicely restored John Deere Van Brunt EN plain-grain drill. Owner of both is Darren Tebbitt of Haddenham, Cambs, who organized the first UK EXPO.

James Coward plowing with his "BW," Serial No. 122,242, and 4B 2-bottom plow. The 3/4 rear view emphasizes the sleek lines of the Model "BW."

The 2-Cylinder Era, Part 1: 1893-1951

Horticulture Needs Met

As early as 1936 the company had perceived a demand by small farmers and horticulturalists for a tractor which would enable them to mechanize their holding. Initially, experimental models were built in the Wagon Works in Moline, using an 8-horsepower Novo engine.

The success of these, designated the Model "Y" with some 24 built, encouraged the further production of an updated version called the 62. Some 79 were built in the summer of 1937, fitted with a vertical 2-cylinder Hercules engine in place of the Novo.

Again these proved acceptable, so a production line was set up and nearly 4,000 tractors, now called the Model "L," were built between 1937 and 1939. In that year the Dreyfuss styling was added, and the models continued until the summer of 1941 when Deere replaced the Hercules engine with one of their own.

This followed the introduction the previous year of the LA, with 14 hp against the 10 horsepower of the "L" and 24-inch cast rear wheels replacing the 22-inch pressed steel of the earlier model.

An archives photo of the original 1936 Model "Y" tractor fitted with Hercules 2-cylinder side-valve engine.

Jack Kreeger's reproduction Model "Y" with Novo engine and built from original blueprints.

With the real thing as its backdrop, a pedal version of the "L" is even complete with sunshade.

This Model "L" crawler, Serial No. 101, was exhibited at the Mt. Pleasant show in 1984 and looked good enough to have been a production unit.

A group photo taken at the first EXPO showing, clockwise from left lower, a 62, unstyled "L," and styled "L," "LI," and "LA," showing the development over five years of Deere's smallest 2-cylinder model. The reproduction "Y" is in the background.

67

The 2-Cylinder Era, Part 1: 1893-1951

Largest Row-Crop Model Introduced

Inevitably the larger farmers of corn and beans demanded a row-crop tractor of similar power to those of their grain-growing cousins, resulting in the introduction in 1937 of the 36-horsepower 3-plow Model "G." Initially it was fitted with a radiator too small to cope with its cooling requirements, but this was soon rectified, and a comparison of the two can be seen from the photo.

In its unstyled form, the "G" was never offered with either single-front wheel or wide-front. In 1941 Deere decided to adopt Dreyfuss styling for the model and fit it with a 6-speed transmission at the same time. Wartime restrictions were by then in force and the government refused the company permission to increase the price. As a result, the model name was changed to "GM" to cover this, although the serial number still showed as G-13,000 up.

With the withdrawal of restrictions the model immediately reverted to "G" from 23,000 serial number, although continuing in styled form with pan seat and battery between the radiator and engine as on the "GM," if fitted with lights or electric starting.

It was not until serial number 26,000 that the model was finally brought into line with the late style Models "A" and "B" and given the armchair seat with batteries beneath. The main frame was not changed to pressed steel as in the other models, but the single-front wheel and wide-axle versions were offered, theoretically from 13,000 up.

Illustrating the small (original) and large radiator versions of the unstyled "G." Note the gap under the steering rod on the former and the small indent in the top radiator tank of the latter.

Identical in appearance to the wartime "GM" but restored to the Model "G" name, this example Serial No. 24,081 was the first of this series seen by the author; it is owned by Arthur Waechter of Maybee, Michigan. The muffler is not original.

The later type of unstyled "G," Serial No. 7,890, with cast rear wheels and pressed-steel fronts.

A number of "GN" were imported to England in the late 1940s. With a few Model "D"'s they were the last 2-cylinder tractors to reach the U.K., the revaluation of the pound sterling against the dollar preventing any further imports until the advent of the New Generation. The "GN" illustrated at a U.S. show has mid-mounted planting equipment.

The tractor which really was . . . A "GW," Serial No. 33,055, at one time part of the author's collection, seen at the Fairford Show in Gloucestershire, August 23, 1992.

The tractor that might have been . . . A standard "G" built by Louis Bartley of Illinois City, Illinois.

69

The 2-Cylinder Era, Part 1: 1893-1951

Smallest 2-Cylinder Horizontal Model

Having satisfied the top end of the row-crop market, the next requirement was for a tractor smaller than the "B," and it was announced in 1939 as the Model "H." Although preproduction models were built without styling, all those marketed had similar appearance to their two larger equivalents.

In 1940 a single-front-wheel option was offered, the "HN," but not a wide front as with the "A" and "B." For one year the "HNH" and "HWH" were supplied, chiefly to satisfy a demand in California, but wartime restrictions ended this option, and it was not resumed. The final option which was exercised by a number of customers was electric starting and lighting.

Two types of front axle were available for the "HWH"; the narrow center section on "HWH," Serial No. 32,012, allowed a narrower setting for certain row crops. Another of the Keller collection, this "HWH" has optional fenders which are peculiar to the "H" series.

This "HWH," Serial No. 35,402, has the alternative wide center as in the composite photo. Both examples here were to be seen at EXPO I.

A composite picture taken in the grounds of the company's headquarters showing, from right the "HN," "H," "HWH," and "HNH." These tractors were subsequently on show on the display floor at the Administrative Center.

The 2-Cylinder Era, Part 1: 1893-1951

Models "A" and "B" Modernized

The final versions of the most popular models until this time, the "A" and "B," were introduced in 1947 with the adoption of pressed-steel frames, enclosed flywheel for standard electric starting, battery under the armchair seat, the option of all-fuel or high-compression gas engines, Roll-O-Matic front wheels, and Powr-Trol.

Electric starting allowed both the "A" and "G" to be offered in genuine high-crop form as the "AH" and "GH."

Electric-start late-type "A," Serial No. 597,364, is seen at a vintage tractor sale in England near Godalming, Surrey, on June 2, 1990.

The height of the Layhers' "GH," Serial No. 63,288, is well illustrated here with Lester standing alongside. A similar "AH" was also available and they have one in their collection.

The late type "AW" tractors had a 4-stud axle fixing to allow interchangeability with single- or twin-wheel models. This tractor, seen near Spokane, Washington, has a 2100 tool carrier for quick coupling to its plow.

A number of late "A"s were brought to the U.K with single front wheels in the late 1940s, all with the larger 16-in. front wheel, some with 38-in. rears, others with 42 in. Correct size for the 38-in. rear was the 10-in. front shown, keeping the tractor level.

At the sale organized to coincide with EXPO II in 1990, this "BWH," Serial No. 228,476, on 42-in. rears and in immaculate condition made $3,350.

The 2-Cylinder Era, Part 1: 1893-1951

New Vertical 2-Cylinder Models from New Factory

Another 1947 introduction was the Model "M" from a new factory built on the banks of the Mississippi at Dubuque. The new model replaced the "H" and "L/LA" series and was intended to answer the competition of the small grey Ferguson.

As the only plowman in the visiting party from the United Kingdom, the author was detailed to demonstrate the new tractor with 2-bottom mounted plow at the factory in the fall of 1947.

The "M" was supplied with a new 2-cylinder vertical gas engine and Touch-O-Matic hydraulics, electric starting and PTO as standard, with lights and pulley as options.

Two years later the series was extended to include a tricycle version, the "MT" with single-front or wide-axle options, an "MI" industrial for highway use, and the "MC" crawler, which replaced the "BO"-Lindeman, Deere having acquired the Yakima, Washington, factory in 1946.

This August 1944 photo shows an "X69" or preproduction Model "M" tractor with a 5-ft cut 10AW combine at Geneseo, Illinois, some three years before the "M" was announced.

This restored "MTN," Serial No. 20,504, resides in Holland and is part of the collection of Piet Peper of Wieringerwaard.

A nicely restored "MT" complete with mid-mounted toolbar and rear tire-mark remover at the Boswell Show, Indiana.

No Model "M" tractors were imported into the United Kingdom due to the ready availability of the home-produced Ferguson and the lack of foreign currency. Several were imported to Southern Ireland, and the example shown, Serial No. 14,021 was purchased there for the author's collection in 1962 and so remained until 1988, when it was purchased by its present owner, Graham Ellis of Chagford, Devon. The photo was taken before it was painted (for more information see chapter 1).

XMT 01 with single front wheel pictured in the studio in August 1947.

James Coward's "MC," Serial No. 16,141, had a man-size job when it was in charge of Ron Knight's restored IH 31T combine at the Stamford, Lincs, working weekend in the autumn of 1993.

The 2-Cylinder Era, Part 1: 1893-1951

Deere's First Diesel

An event which had been promised for a long time finally occurred in 1949 with the introduction of the company's first diesel model. The requirement for a larger tractor than the veteran "D" had been obvious since the end of the war, and the Model "R" solved this problem.

Equipped with a 2-cylinder main engine, a 2-cylinder horizontally-opposed starting motor, itself started electrically, this 7.4-ton 45-horsepower tractor soon proved popular with large grain growers around the world. In addition, when tested at Nebraska it took the world fuel-economy record.

Only one of these tractors was imported into the British Isles originally, No. 4661 going to a contractor in Dublin, and as soon as it was traded in 1962 was purchased by the author for use on his farm.

The final introduction of the lettered series was the styling of the Models "AR" and "AO," similar to the new style adopted for the "R," and the addition of the two higher gears as on the row-crop models.

Model "MX" pre-"R" at Loredo, Texas, on field tests, suitably camouflaged with Case LA-type hood. The starting motor was built by the Moline Wagon Works, home of the L series.

Heading the line-up at the Peterborough Vintage Club's open day was this beautiful "R," Serial No. 7,945, with 5-furrow 66 plow in tow.

Last of the lettered series to be styled was the "AR." A typical use for these models was to pull an engine-driven 65 combine with pickup attachment in windrowed wheat in Canada.

The last styled "AO" built, Serial No. 284,074, is now the property of Tom Langan of La Crescent, Minn., who purchased it in 1979.

The 2-Cylinder Era, Part 2: 1952-1960

A Swedish Compliment?

In the early 1950s the Swedish company of Gnosjo Mekaniski Werkstad or GMW built a few 2-cylinder tractors based on the later-style John Deere Models "AW" and "BW," designated Models 35 (250 built from 1952) and 25 (220 built from 1955). Most were sold in Sweden but a few went to Finland and Brazil.

The photo shows the similarity of the 35 to the "AW" (on the 25 this was more like the "BW"), with an altered pressed-steel frame, grille, and muffler. The front axle was non-adjustable and the wheels were from a local supplier, but the similarities cannot be denied. They also built a larger diesel Model 45 copied from another European tractor company.

The Numbered Series

In 1952 the long-established Models "A" and "B," after nearly 20 years in the line, were replaced with the Models 60 and 50, respectively. Styled like the "R," "AR," and "AO," they included many new features. Gone was the splined rear axle for rear-wheel adjustment and in its place was a keyed hub with rack-and-pinion system to move the heavy cast rear wheels.

The engines featured duplex carburetors, hot and cold manifolds with cyclonic-fuel intake, and belt-driven water pump. A "live" PTO shaft meant continuous power was available to drawn machines, allowing much larger capacity combines, forage harvesters, balers, and other similar machines to be used without auxiliary engines. All the previous model options were continued.

Johannes Calamnius is at home in Sweden with this GMW 35, Serial No. 584, the property of Uno Johansson of Vedum, Sweden.

Another model which might have been . . . A 50 "standard," the creation of Barry Stelford of Urbana, Illinois.

A really neat outfit, this 50 gasoline tractor is pulling both a PTO-driven 25 combine and its attendant grain trailer.

This 60, Serial No. 39,211, with gasoline engine, Roll-O-Matic front axle, power steering, and complete with sunshade is pictured near Mankato, Minnesota.

A 50 row-crop with wide front is transporting a 43 PTO sheller to its next job.

79

The 2-Cylinder Era, Part 2: 1952-1960

Dubuque Models Join the Line

Among the many options available on the Models 50 and 60 were a rear exhaust system for use in low buildings, "Live" high-pressure Powr-Trol hydraulic, Quick-Change wheel tread, and interchangeable front-end assemblies. The 800 hitch was a first attempt to get around restrictions on existing patents and licenses operating at that time.

During the next year, 1953, Dubuque followed Waterloo with the 40 series replacing the "M," the "G" became the 70 series, and LP gas became a fuel option, particularly for the Southern states, where it was a cheap fuel source.

Plowing in a crop of alfalfa with a 3-furrow mounted plow, this 40RCU is built lower than the wide-front row-crop model. It was also known as a Two-Row Utility.

❶ This early 60 standard, Serial No. 26,639, with low seat position like the styled Model "AR" it replaced, has original tires and is pictured at Evansville, Indiana.

❷ The later 60 standard, Serial No. 46,567, has the high seat arrangement which continued through the 620 series—another EXPO I shot.

❸ This 60 Hi-Crop with all-fuel engine is a rare bird, 136 were built, though the LP version was even more rare, with only 15 examples.

This studio photo taken in December 1952 shows the 40T with its wide front axle in a wide setting.

A November 17, 1952, studio photo of a new 40 tricycle tractor equipped with a 4200 mid-mounted cultivator.

This 40C crawler at the first EXPO is equipped with the reversible Lindeman blade for front or rear use, essentially only suitable for farm work.

Another studio photo of the 40C with 5-roller track frame, radiator and light guard, and remote hydraulic cylinder.

The 2-Cylinder Era, Part 2: 1952-1960

Deere's First Diesel Row-Crop Model

In the fall of 1953 the company introduced its first diesel row-crop tractor, the 70D, and took the opportunity to replace the starting engine used on the "R" with a V-4 high-speed gasoline-driven unit. The new model wrested the world fuel economy title from the "R" in its Nebraska Test No. 528.

One other model change occurred in 1954 when the 60 standard tractor was altered to a higher-clearance style like the larger 70 standard.

It was not until 1955 that the "R" was finally replaced with the 80, which was equipped with full factory-installed power steering, offered first on the 50, 60, and 70 the previous year.

This 70, Serial No. 41,121, with gasoline engine, Roll-O-Matic front, and power steering is pictured near Mankato, Minnesota.

The only gasoline-engined 70S in England, Serial No. 23,417, on arrival in Suffolk on August 18, 1989, after shipment from Lyle Dumont, Sigourney, Iowa.

Making an interesting comparison with the previous photo, this 70D, Serial No. 38,786, is a nicely restored example of Deere's first row-crop diesel model and is complete with optional power steering. Note the top drive to the flywheel on the diesel model.

Studio picture of a 70D row-crop with wide front, taken in April 1955.

Another April 1955 photo of a 70 diesel Hi-Crop tractor at work with 71 Hi-Crop hitch and 72 cane plow. Note the door in the rear of the hood which gives access to the gasoline tank.

Gary Koop of Waverly, Iowa, is the fortunate owner of the first two production 80s, Serial Nos. 8,000,001 and 8,000,002. Number 1 is nearest the camera, and is in its original ex-factory condition; Gary is standing in front of Number 2, at EXPO III.

The 2-Cylinder Era, Part 2: 1952-1960

A Power Increase of 20%

By 1956 the demand from farmers for increased power led to the introduction of the 20 series with approximately 20 percent more horsepower. The 420 models from Dubuque were the first of the new line, originally in all-green livery like their predecessors.

It was soon decided to take advantage of the new line to modernize their looks and appeal by painting the center and front panels of the hood yellow. This gave the new line a distinctive look, the most attractive of all in the eyes of some collectors.

The introduction of these new models produced a demand for a tractor of lower power than the 420, so the 320 was introduced, which was effectively the old 40 with the new styling.

The Waterloo-built tractors had power steering as standard, and the Float-Ride seat could be adjusted for operator weight. Most important of the new specifications was Custom Powr-Trol, which gave more accurate implement depth control and improved grip through automatic weight transfer.

In the new series the 420C crawler provided tracks of a more robust design, and the continued option of a 4- or 5-roller track frame.

With the 20% power increase over earlier models of the 20 series, a need for a tractor of the same horsepower as the Model 40 resulted in the introduction of the 320. Two versions were offered, the standard and the utility shown here.

The uprated 40 became the 420 and is seen here in its Utility model version at a sale at Waterloo, Iowa, on July 2, 1990.

A 420 row-crop utility tractor makes light work of planting with a 23C mounted planter on a 4262 cultivator in March 1957.

This 420C and dozer shown at the 1992 EXPO indicated a future industrial application; it was owned by Jim Proctor from distant Pennsylvania.

Lant Elrod's "Florida Gold" painting of the orchard version of the 620 tractor which was EXPO III's theme model.

The 2-Cylinder Era, Part 2: 1952-1960

A 620 row-crop tractor, Serial No. 10,936, on show at the first EXPO in 1987.

In charge of an engine-driven 65 combine picking up swathed wheat, this 620W with wide front has a fairly easy time.

Single-front-wheel 520N planting with a 74-76 Beet and Bean planter.

This 620 standard, Serial No. 9,812, is pictured at the first EXPO in Waterloo.

A job for a man-size tractor. This 720 gasoline-engined row-crop model copes easily with a 5-furrow drawn plow.

The 2-Cylinder Era, Part 2: 1952-1960

The Largest 2-Cylinder Tractor

The 820 proved to be the most powerful 2-cylinder tractor produced by Deere, giving 75.6 brake horsepower at Nebraska. The 30 series were never tested there, since there were no mechanical changes between the two series.

Robert Carrico of Madison, Kentucky, restored this beautiful 720 diesel standard tractor.

A studio photo of a gasoline-powered 720 Hi-crop.

88

A contrast in styles—Deere's largest 2-cylinder models from 1949 to 1957, the "R," 80, and 820, are shown in this montage.

With a 5-bottom 77H plow attached, this 820 diesel tractor seen at EXPO III was the property of Richard Miller from Ohio. A WA14 makes an interesting backdrop.

The 2-Cylinder Era, Part 2: 1952-1960

Last 2-Cylinder Series Introduced

In 1958 the final 2-cylinder series appeared but this was really a styling exercise, with larger yellow side panels, a sloping steering wheel and instrument panel, and fenders which would be copied on the soon to be announced multi-cylinder New Generation of tractors.

The whole 20 series line was repeated in the 30 series. For some reason this series is especially popular with collectors (maybe it is simply the fact that they were the last 2-cylinder series built in the United States).

Perhaps Daniel O'Brien of Barnet, Vermont, in a *Green Magazine* article, put it best:

"I studied them (the 30 series) for hours, my eyes transfixed by the sensually pleasing green and yellow hoods with the characteristic slant down the sides. The rounded front grill and dual headlight fenders gave the tractors a finished look like a highly polished emerald.

The styling of the 30 series was just plain eye catching, everything "fit" was correct in proportion. Deere was well aware of the aesthetic enhancements that came from the upgrade from 20 to 30 series tractors. It was the last hurrah to a phenomenal engineering marvel that spanned parts of five decades. Deere paid tribute, literally, to the two cylinders by allowing them to enter the slip stream of history in style."

First representative of the restyled 30 series is this 330 standard tractor, Serial No. 330,286, on the day before the Van Buren, Michigan, Show on September 7, 1989.

The lower-built 430RCU awaits a buyer at Dennis Polk's sale on August 17, 1984. In due course Serial No. 158,898 made $1,875.

430T tricycle tractor with 25 engine-driven combine with draper pickup attachment at EXPO III.

Seen on July 25, 1990, this 430HC makes an attractive picture.

A 430C with optional 5-roller track frame and radiator guard shows its ability to turn on a dime.

A 430T-N with single front wheel is hauling a load of corn cobs in a 1064 wagon back to its home base in November 1958.

91

The 2-Cylinder Era, Part 2: 1952-1960

In June 1958, a 530 prepares hay for a baler with an 896 semi-integral side delivery rake.

Another EXPO exhibit, this 530 has the usual wide front, wrap-around front weight, and an integral plow.

Richard Lester Jr's 630 standard with downswept exhaust from Delaware heads a lineup with Robert Hampton's 730 Hi-Crop at EXPO III.

In May 1958 the 45 loader-equipped 730 filled a Model W PTO-driven manure distributor.

A 630RCW, Serial No. 10,785, with wide-front and 3-point hitch has a twin-front 630RC along side at Chad der Ploeg's, Sully, Iowa.

Frank's pride and joy! Frank Rochawiak from Southgate, Michigan, loves this 630S more than his wife, Trish—or so she jokingly says.

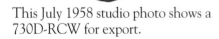

This July 1958 studio photo shows a 730D-RCW for export.

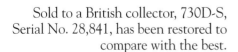

Sold to a British collector, 730D-S, Serial No. 28,841, has been restored to compare with the best.

The 2-Cylinder Era, Part 2: 1952-1960

A Small Diesel Model Ends 2-Cylinder Era

Apart from the option offered with the 730 and 830 diesels of pony-engine or direct electric starting, the last 2-cylinder model to appear was Deere's first small diesel tractor. Again the competition demanded a response in the 30-horsepower size and the 435, a 430 fitted with a GM 2-cycle 2-cylinder diesel engine, was the result.

In the rapidly growing industrial field the new 440 wheel and crawler tractors were similarly equipped, except in Europe, where Mannheim fitted a Perkins 3-cylinder engine instead of the GM. In a later chapter other 2-cylinder developments in Argentina will be discussed.

Electric-start 830, Serial No. 5,393, was shipped from Spokane, Washington, to England in 1992, and has since gone to a German collector, Albert Knoth of Feilbingert, not far from Mannheim.

The last of the 2-cylinder industrial designs was offered in both wheel and crawler form. Wheeled Model 440, Serial No. 450,616, complete with sunshade is loaded at EXPO ready to return to its home in Illinois.

Purchased from one of the world's largest collectors of 2-cylinder John Deere tractors, Don Dufner, Buxton, North Dakota, and this 830 was shipped to England in 1990. Serial No. 2,719 has been beautifully restored by its new owner, David Lee of Hunstanton, Norfolk.

Latest of various specials built by Don Dufner, this twin 830 is used by him on his "All-Two-Cylinder" farming operation at Buxton, North Dakota. Note the Sound-Gard body—is this the only 2-cylinder-based tractor so equipped?—and the position of the second tractor's radiator. The air intake can just be seen at the corner of the cab, following modern practice.

Jim Proctor's 840, Serial No. 840,387, with Hancock self-loading scraper makes an impressive exhibit at EXPO III. Note the offset operator's position to allow direct connection for the scraper gooseneck. One of the new 60 series articulated models is seen in the background.

The only 435 in the U.K., Serial No. 435,103, is the property of George Wisener of Mauchline in Scotland. It is seen at the EXPO of the British branch of the Two-Cylinder Club.

Multi-Cylinder Models Replace the 2-Cylinder Line

The year 1960 will go down in history as the time when Deere & Company took a giant leap forward in the development of the modern tractor. The new Waterloo models announced in Dallas on August 29, 1960, were several years ahead of the competition, and became classics in their field.

Deere & Company also introduced the new concept of high horsepower-to-weight ratio which was to become the norm for the industry, plus closed-center hydraulics, lower-link sensing, and hydraulic power brakes—all industry firsts.

The 6-cylinder 4010, with its 4-cylinder stablemate the 3010, led the way, followed two years later by the 5010, the world's first wheel tractor with over 100 PTO and drawbar horsepower. It also introduced Category 3 linkage to cope with this power. The 5010 was Deere's first tractor with 1,000-rpm-only PTO.

The model numbering system adopted for the New Generation tractors had been anticipated the previous year with the announcement of the 215-horsepower 8010 4-wheel-drive articulated tractor introduced to dealers and the public at Marshaltown, Iowa.

The 3010 and 4010 were available as row-crop models with four alternative front-wheel options, and as standard or wheatland tractors. The 3010 could also be ordered as a row-crop utility or an orchard model, while the 4010 had an alternative Hi-Crop version.

Bill Hewitt, company chairman, seen at the controls of one of the first 8010 tractors. The tractor shows its flexibility in this photo.

A 4010 with gasoline engine is doing a good job in charge of a No. 12 forage harvester cutting, chopping, and loading alfalfa. This model forage harvester was popular in the United Kingdom

Kenneth Becker from Nebraska was allowed to show his 3010 and 4010 diesel tractors at the Two-Cylinder EXPO III, because they were the first production example of each model, both Serial No. 1,000.

The depth of plowing can be judged by the tractor wheels in the furrow and since this wide-front 4010D is only pulling a 3-bottom plow. All the 4010 tractors imported into the United Kingdom were similar diesel models with wide front.

Studio photo of the 5010 in its original condition.

Multi-Cylinder Models Replace the 2-Cylinder Line

Two smaller 4-cylinder models from Dubuque, the 1010 and 2010, were announced in Dallas at the same time as the two Waterloo tractors. The former was available in 10 styles including seven row-crop models, an orchard version, and two crawlers, and with choice of gasoline or diesel engines.

The 2010, with styling more closely linked to the Waterloo models, was offered in six row-crop styles, a Hi-Crop, and in the following year a crawler, which could be said to have true industrial applications. In addition to gasoline and diesel engines, the 2010 joined the larger models with an LP-gas option.

Studio photo of the 1010 tricycle row-crop tractor with gasoline engine.

One of the smallest of the New Generation of tractors, this 1010 row-crop utility diesel is pulling a 25B unit planter.

A rare 2010 Hi-Crop tractor with LP-gas engine owned by Robert Dufel of Hudson, Iowa.

This 2010 tricycle row-crop model has the optional gasoline engine. Note the flat-top fenders like the larger models and unlike the 1010 tricycle.

Multi-Cylinder Models Replace the 2-Cylinder Line

20 Series from Waterloo

After three years experience in the field, the 3010 and 4010 were replaced by the new 20 series—the 3020 and 4020. One reason for the change, in addition to the extra power provided, was the announcement of Power Shift, an automatic transmission with 8 forward and 4 reverse speeds available without clutching. An inching pedal was provided for attaching implements.

The 4020 in particular was exactly the tractor farmers were looking for in their quest for efficiency. It became the most popular tractor of its time, ranking as a classic with its famous predecessor, the Model "D."

This 4020 standard diesel tractor is complete with full fenders and platform dust shields and retains an adjustable front axle.

This September 1963 studio photo shows the 4-cylinder gasoline-engined version of the 3020 Hi-Crop model.

A group photo taken on the introduction of the new 20 series tractors showing (front row lower left, 1020, 2020, 3020 and back row left, 2510, 4020, and 5020). The latter four are all row-crop models.

An early 4020 diesel row-crop model with Power Shift and wide front was originally imported into the United Kingdom with the smaller standard-type fenders, but has been restored with the U.S. flat-top type. Serial No. 96,306 is seen at Parsons Bros. near Gloucester on November 16, 1989.

Multi-Cylinder Models Replace the 2-Cylinder Line

World Tractor Designed

The advent of the 20 series from Waterloo created a demand for similar tractors for the smaller farmer, or as second machines on larger farms. The result was the introduction for 1965 of the 3-cylinder 1020 and 4-cylinder 2020 from Dubuque to replace the 1010 and 2010.

Referred to as utility tractors, they included closed-center hydraulics, lower-link sensing, and engage-on-the-go differential as on the larger machines. Both models were available in low, regular, or high styles, and both were offered additionally as orchard models.

A Smaller Row-Crop Model from Waterloo

The new 4-cylinder engine had two counter-rotating balancer shafts, a standard Deere requirement to reduce vibration in 4-cylinder engines, and this allowed the introduction for 1966 of a smaller row-crop tractor than the 3020, the 2510, with all the larger tractor's features.

Built in Waterloo, it was offered with Syncro-Range and Power Shift transmission, power steering, and differential lock, and could be bought with the same choice of four front ends (twin, Roll-O-Matic, single front wheel, or wide front axle), and with gasoline or diesel engine. A Hi-Crop was also available.

An overhead view of the 1020RU and 2020RU tractors, the latter with optional swept-back front axle, and both with downswept exhaust.

This orchard-model 2020 with full citrus fenders shows the filler-cap protection. Note the low headlight position to avoid branches.

A 1020RU equipped with 37 loader and 78 yard scraper is seen loading manure into a 33 PTO-driven spreader hauled by a 2020HU.

A 2020HU equipped with downswept exhaust, adjustable row-crop back axle, ROPS, and a good complement of weights is busy at work with a drawn planter.

A gasoline-engined 2510 row-crop tractor with wide front.

103

Multi-Cylinder Models Replace the 2-Cylinder Line

The announcement of the 5020 to replace the 5010 came in 1966. With an increase in PTO horsepower from 121 to 133, and with improved air intake to the engine, the new model provided the extra power demanded by large grain growers.

In the fall of 1966 its versatility was further extended by the provision of an adjustable front axle, allowing the use of these large machines for row-crop work.

Small Tractor Line Extended

When the Dubuque-designed models were introduced in Europe, several extra models were included in the lineup since the number of small farms demanded this extra coverage. It was not surprising, therefore, when the smallest model, the 31-PTO-horsepower 820, and an intermediate size, the 46-PTO-horsepower 1520, were introduced to the American market in 1968. Both models were 3-cylinder and the latter included all the features of the two original tractors.

Canada imported the European models since they had a price advantage there. As a result, a pilot run of 710 models was introduced having the 4-cylinder 2010 engine, and this was followed by the 36-horsepower 920 and 45-horsepower 1120, Mannheim's equivalent of the 1520. In 1969 the 2120 4-cylinder 70-horsepower model was added to the Canadian line.

A 5020, Serial No. 13,416, recently acquired by John Moore of Knowle, Warwickshire, England. Note the large first front weight, allowing double stacking of add-on weights when heavy integral equipment was used, and the extra pair of headlamps for U.K. road conditions.

A studio photo of the row-crop version of the 5020 equipped with twin rear wheels. Note the different fender style on these models compared with the previous photo.

A regular 820 with swept-back front axle is seen cultivating.

A Canadian 45-hp 1120 is tidying up some ground with a rotary cutter made in Welland, Ontario.

Two 820 tractors make light work of clearing manure from a farmyard; one is equipped with a 37 loader and both have swept-back front axles.

The 20 series tractors supplied from Mannheim for the Canadian market were equipped with shell fenders and lights as shown on this 2120 and the 1120 above.

105

Multi-Cylinder Models Replace the 2-Cylinder Line

Waterloo Tractors Updated and Line Extended

In 1968 the 3020 and 4020 tractors were fitted with refined engines, easily recognizable by the narrow oval muffler in place of the original circular one, a dry-type air cleaner, and 12-volt electrical system. At the same time, a hydrostatic Power Front-Wheel Drive was added to the list of available options. The following year, the power of the 2510 was increased from 54 to 61 horsepower, justifying its new model number 2520.

This 3020 "Classic" tractor, equipped with a 48 loader, is filling a 76 flail spreader, a type common in Europe.

This studio view of the 2520 with gasoline engine and twin-wheel row-crop front shows off the clean lines of this smaller Waterloo model.

The last 4020, diesel tractor, Serial No. 270,288, is now with Deere's archive collection in Moline. It has a factory-fitted cab, an accessory which became increasingly popular before the advent of the Sound-Gard body.

This 4020 Classic, Serial No. 263,524 has been beautifully restored by Roger Perry to its original December 1971 imported condition. The European tractors had standard-type fenders but row-crop operator's platform, lights as supplied with tractors without fenders, and row-crop front axle.

A late 4020 with Power Front-Wheel Drive and cab is plowing with a 100FH flexible drawn chisel plow with synchronized hydraulic depth control.

Multi-Cylinder Models Replace the 2-Cylinder Line

Deere's First Turbocharged Model

Deere's first turbo-built tractor, the 4520 with 122 PTO horsepower, was announced about the same time as another new model, the 4000. The new 4000 was effectively a 4020 engine with a 3020 transmission, having the same power as the former at a lower price.

Super 4020 and New 4620 Greet the 1970s

Late in 1970 a more powerful version of the 4020, but without the extra weight of the 4520, appeared in the shape of the 4320, fitted with a turbocharged version of the former's engine. Giving a 21-percent increase in power to 115 horsepower, it meant the existing 4520 had to be uprated. As the new 4620 it became the first farm tractor to be intercooled as well as turbocharged, another Deere first, with a resulting increase in its power to 135 PTO horsepower.

A used 4520 parked in the Grundy Center (Iowa) Deere dealer's yard emphasizes the rather ungainly appearance of the cab supplied in the late 1960s. The 4520 was Deere's first turbocharged diesel model.

The 4000 was a lower priced version of the 4020, being basically a 4010 with a 4020 engine. It is seen here chopping corn stalk residue with a 27 Flail Shredder.

108

On a cool 1972 fall day in Canada the 4620 operator was kept comfortable by his factory-built cab while harvesting flax with an engine-driven 106 combine.

Field view of a new 4320 diesel tractor. The large oval muffler fitted on all turbocharged models is evident in this photo.

Left-side view of a standard turbocharged and intercooled 4620 with large fenders, front platform shields, and adjustable front axle.

109

Multi-Cylinder Models Replace the 2-Cylinder Line

Deere Returns to the 4-Wheel-Drive Market

Not content with these developments, the company announced a new articulated 4-wheel-drive model, the 7020. Two years before, in 1969, arrangements had been made with Warners to market their WA-14 and WA-17, suitably restyled, as an interim measure while their own machine was perfected. These giants had 225 and 280 flywheel, 178 and 220 drawbar horsepower, respectively. The new 7020 used a turbocharged and intercooled 145-horsepower engine. The following year the second Deere 4WD, the 7520, joined the line with a larger 175-horsepower engine.

The introduction of the new engine for the 7520 allowed the 5020 to be updated to the 6030. It was the first John Deere tractor to be offered with the choice of two engines, either the original naturally aspirated 141-horsepower type or the turbocharged and intercooled 175-horsepower model. Again the 6030 could be sold in standard or row-crop form and fitted with either single or dual rear wheels, but it retained the original 20 series styling.

A nicely restored 8020, Serial No. 1,092, makes an interesting contrast with the 2-cylinder tractors on show at the first EXPO in Waterloo, Iowa.

Deere's interim articulated 4-wheel-drive tractors in the late 1960s were restyled Warner 225-engine-hp WA-14 and 280-hp WA-17 models. Darrel Fischer's restored WA-14 is pictured at EXPO III in 1992.

This 175-hp 6030 dwarfs the Lincoln car alongside on a farm near Regina, Saskatchewan, in 1972. The 6030 retained the 20 series styling throughout.

A 7020 fitted with twin wheels illustrates the first Waterloo-built articulated 4-wheel-drive since the 100 8010 and 8020 models were built a decade earlier.

The 7520 was externally similar to the 7020 but had an extra 34 hp with its larger and slower-governed engine, 2,100 rpm compared with 2,200 on the 7020.

Multi-Cylinder Models Replace the 2-Cylinder Line

Generation II

Late in 1972 the Waterloo-built tractors took another leap ahead of the competition. They appeared with completely new styling and the option of either Sound-Gard body, as the new safety cab was known, with under 85 dB(A), or a 4-post Roll-Gard ROPS. The four models were the 80-PTO-horsepower 4030; the 100-horsepower 4230; the turbocharged 125-horsepower 4430, set to become the most popular model in the line; and largest of the line, the 4630 with 150 PTO horsepower, turbocharged and intercooled.

The new tractors, known as Generation II because of their dramatic innovations, were an instant success. The new features included new transmissions, hydraulically controlled Perma-Clutch, a virtual lifetime wet-type clutch, and the considerable advance in safety and comfort for the operator.

Initially it was anticipated that some 40% of orders would be with the new cab, but in the end a large proportion of the new line was ordered with it fitted.

The 4030 with the new-style 4-post ROPS adapted from the Sound-Gard body still sports a radio.

Hydrostatic Power Front-Wheel Drive was an option on all the Generation II models.

112

Another option was the Hi-Crop model, available as either the 4230 shown here or the 4430.

Field view of an open-station low-profile 4230, the direct opposite of the previous photo; these were sold mainly in Mexico, Argentina, and similar overseas markets.

Restored 4630 with European lights—a single unit under each fender and an extra pair by the nose of the tractor. The 4630 was not legal for use on U.K. roads, as it was not equipped with an independent hand-operated brake.

Multi-Cylinder Models Replace the 2-Cylinder Line

30 Series Extended

Another model to retain the early styling, although upgraded to 30 series, was the 4-cylinder 2030 in 1972. Initially built in Dubuque, this model was also built in Mannheim from 1974, with a separate serial number series. It had a 26% torque reserve, a high figure for a utility tractor.

In 1973, for the 1974 model year, three other utility tractors were added to the U.S. line, still with the early styling: the 830 with 35 horsepower and the 1530 45 horsepower, both built in Mannheim, and the powerful Dubuque-built 2630 with 70 PTO horsepower. With three PTO options, 540-rpm as standard and 540/1,000-rpm rear optional plus a 1,000-rpm mid-mounted option in addition, all the PTO requirements were covered; a Quik-Coupler hitch was another option.

All four models in this line had sloping, non-reflective dash panels and the use of 2-post Roll-Gard protection was encouraged; all but the smallest had closed-center hydraulics with lower-link sensing. The 830 and 1530 had 3-cylinder engines, the 2030 and 2630 4-cylinder, with balancer shafts to smooth out vibration.

With the ever-increasing demand for more power it was to be expected that the 4-wheel-drive models should be updated. In 1975 they received the new styling, and the 8430 and 8630 were announced with 178 and 225 PTO horsepower, respectively.

This 2030LU pulls a fully equipped drawn planting rig in the days before ROPS was the standard alternative to a cab.

Original-style 2630 with ROPS and wind-out rear wheels; this model was only built in Dubuque, unlike many of the smaller models which were built in Mannheim.

Posed together, the 8430 and 8630 were photographed for the front cover of their sales brochure in 1976.

Multi-Cylinder Models Replace the 2-Cylinder Line

Canada Acquires 30 Series from Mannheim

The European 30 series line was restyled to match the Waterloo-built tractors late in 1975. Since Canada's under-100-horsepower tractors were supplied by Mannheim, the only 30 series models seen there in the old style were the 1830, 2130, and a few 3130s in the old style.

The 36-horsepower 920 and 45-horsepower 1120 were not updated until the new styling was introduced, when they were replaced by the 40-horsepower 1030 and 50-horsepower 1630, respectively, the latter the equivalent to the U.S. 1530.

The Mannheim 2030 became the 1830 in Canada to avoid confusion with the Dubuque-built U.S. model. The 2130, which was the equivalent in power to the 2630, had a turbocharged 239-cubic-inch engine instead of the latter's 276-cubic-inch naturally aspirated version. All models had the American-style shell or row-crop fenders in place of the European type.

The 80-horsepower 6-cylinder 3130 was introduced in Canada as a lower-cost option to the 4030.

Waiting to go planting, this early-style 1830 has a 7000 planter in tow in a typical North American farmyard.

Making an interesting comparison with the original-style 2130, the new-style 2130 is similarly equipped.

An impression of power is conveyed by this original-style 3130 pulling a large set of disk harrows in its Canadian trim.

This original-style 2130 has shell fenders and lighting as supplied for the Canadian market.

This 3130 with adjustable rear axle, ROPS, and flat-top fenders is equipped with a 148 front loader and bucket for manure removal on this stock farm

117

New Styling Adopted Worldwide

The 40 Series Utility Line

The new U.S. 40 series utility tractors announced in 1975 for the 1976 season came from two sources, the 3-cylinder models from Mannheim and the 4-cylinder from Dubuque. While the European 2040 and 2240 tractors had about 5 horsepower more than the 830 and 1530 they replaced, the U.S.-built models 2440 and 2640 remained the same in power as the 2030 and 2630.

In addition to the new styling, the most obvious difference in appearance was the new standard of the Roll-Gard rollover protective structure. Besides the standard models, the 2240 was available in both orchard and vineyard form, built low and narrow for these specialized operations.

The following year the Mannheim-built 6-cylinder 80-PTO-horsepower 2840 was added to The Long Green Line, with its 12-forward-speed 6-reverse-speed transmission and Hi-Lo as standard.

The Japanese Connection

Late in 1977 agreement was finally reached with Yanmar to produce a line of under-40-horsepower tractors, and the first two, the 22-horsepower 850 and 27-horsepower 950, were introduced. They were advertised as "Little Big Tractors" since they were small but had big-tractor features.

Both were fitted with 3-cylinder engines of Deere design, 8 forward and 2 reverse speeds, MFWD as an option, differential lock, 540-rpm PTO with overrunning clutch, and Category 1 3-point hitch.

❶ Prepared for bad weather, this 2440 has a Weather Enclosure option added to its ROPS.

❷ A 750 with MFWD is equipped with 67 front loader and rear-mounted backhoe in the display area at the Administrative Center.

❸ The three middle-of-the-range Yanmar models, all ROPS equipped; the 850 and 950 2-wheel drive and the 1050 with MFWD.

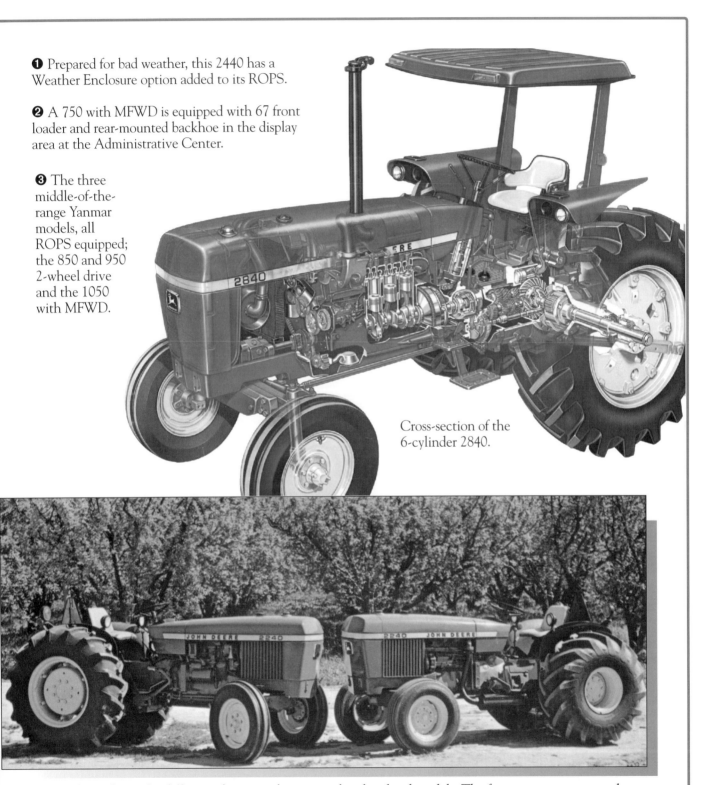

Cross-section of the 6-cylinder 2840.

This photo shows the difference between the vineyard and orchard models. The former are narrower as they have 14.9-24 rear tires; the latter have 18.4-16.1.

119

New Styling Adopted Worldwide

In 1979 the Yanmar line was extended with a larger 3-cylinder model, the 1050, and in 1981 with two smaller ones, the 650 and 750. These latter were sold chiefly by the grounds care products dealers. The next year the 1250, still with three cylinders, was introduced with 40 PTO horsepower. A full line of integral agricultural and grounds maintenance equipment was offered for all models.

The Iron Horses Announced

Late in 1977 the company introduced a new line of five row-crop tractors built in Waterloo for the 1978 season. With more powerful engines, increased drawbar pull, and greater hitch lift capacity, they represented another forward advance in tractor power.

The 4040 and 4240 had naturally aspirated engines giving 90 and 110 PTO horsepower, the 4440 had a turbocharged engine giving 130 PTO horsepower, and the 156-PTO-horsepower 4640 and completely new 180-PTO-horsepower 4840 both had turbocharged and intercooled power units.

All five models had HydraCushioned seat suspension and the new cabs were quieter (under 80 dB(A) sound level), with the 4640 achieving the best reading to date at Nebraska with 77.5 dB(A).

4-Wheel-Drive Models Updated

For 1979 the two articulated models were updated to conform to the other 40 series tractors, with slight increase in power but many internal refinements. Among others was the option of front and rear hydraulic differential locks, increased rockshaft capacity, and up to four remote hydraulic outlets.

Useful occupation for a 1250, this example is tidying up a pasture with a 506 rotary cutter.

An overhead view of a 4640 with twin rear wheels planting with a 7000 series Max-Emerge integral planter.

A 1250-MFWD is hard at work plowing deep with a 3-bottom mounted plow. This photo makes an interesting comparison with the previous 2-wheel-drive 1250.

This 4040, Serial No. 11,759, was delivered to Jim Birk in Hutchinson, Minnesota on October 1, 1981, and cost $33,000. It has the convertible front end, three remote hydraulic outlets, and a Quick-Coupler hitch. Jim's sister, Jayne, joined him for this photo.

A studio photo showing the new 4840, largest size of Waterloo-built row-crop tractor, fitted with the popular twin rear wheels.

New Styling Adopted Worldwide

A new Investigator warning system monitored most of the important engine and transmission functions, giving both sound and visual signals warning of any problems.

Utility Models Restyled

Five utility models were revamped to match the row-crop tractors in the 1980 model year. The hoods were raised towards the back and the steering column repositioned, allowing the option of Sound-Gard bodies, while the 2840 became the 2940. All models tested slightly higher in power, and mechanical front-wheel drive was offered on the Mannheim-built models, 2040, 2240, and 2940. The 2940 now had a new top-shaft-synchronized (TSS) transmission with Hi-Lo shift giving 16 forward, 8 reverse speeds. The company extended the warranty on these tractors to two years or 1,500 hours—whichever came first.

Canada Acquires 40 New Series

With the introduction of the modified 40 series in Europe and the States, it was Canada's turn to change models. In their case, the units were sourced from Mannheim and they introduced the 3-cylinder 44-horsepower 1040 and 50-horsepower 1140 orchard or vineyard models, the 4-cylinder 55-horsepower 1640, 60-horsepower 1840, and 70-horsepower turbocharged 2140, and 6-cylinder 80-horsepower 3140.

Since they were designed to do more work in a given time they were labeled the "Schedule Masters." Canada also marketed the Yanmar 50 series models.

The new styling adopted in 1980 for the 40 series utility tractors allowed the Sound-Gard body to be offered as an option. The hood was raised to the rear instead of sloping down, to match the front aperture of the cab.

A rural hayfield setting with a 2940 baling alfalfa with a 327 baler equipped with bale ejector.

Hard at work, this 2940 2-wheel-drive tractor is equipped with 2-post ROPS canopy, and flat-top fenders.

Studio view of 1640 fitted with 240 front loader, ROPS and canopy, and fitted with Canadian-style fenders and lighting. Note the contrast with the 2940 in the previous photo.

This studio portrait shows the Canadian equivalent of the U.S. 2940, the 6-cylinder 3140 with MFWD and Sound-Gard body.

New Styling Adopted Worldwide

50 Series Have Caster/Action MFWD Option

In the early 1980s the company announced the longest new line of tractors in its history. From Waterloo each of the five 40 series row-crop models were replaced with models of an extra 10 horsepower at the PTO.

The most significant innovation was the introduction of a mechanical front-wheel drive (MFWD), optional on the four smaller models but standard on the largest, the 190-horsepower 4850. This new type of front axle had a 13-degree caster on the front wheels, allowing a much tighter turning radius than had been possible with previous front-wheel-drive options.

A new 15-speed Power Shift transmission and a quieter Sound-Gard body were among other refinements. The 4050 broke the record as the quietest tractor ever tested at Nebraska, while the 4850 set the fuel-efficiency record for tractors over 70 horsepower.

The Efficiency Experts 45 to 85 Horsepower

The economic climate in the early part of the 1980s demanded efficient tractors, and the result was the announcement of the new under-100-horsepower 50 series models. From the 2150 of 45 horsepower to the 85-horsepower 2950, all were now made in Mannheim, while Dubuque became an industrial-line plant. The top-shaft-synchronized transmission (TSS) introduced on the 2940 was added for all models, allowing on-the-go shifting within gear ranges. The Sound-Gard body was now available on all models except the 2150.

A 4050-MFWD equipped with rear twins by an outside supplier is rotary cultivating near Louth, Lincolnshire, England, on August 25, 1990.

Robert Dufel of Hudson, Iowa, has equipped his 4250 with an extra fuel tank and homemade front mudguards. With two trailers it waits for the combine on September 1, 1989.

The five Waterloo-built 50 series models, four with MFWD: 4050, 4450, 4650, and 4850, the latter two with twin rears, and the 4250 in 2-wheel-drive mode. The 4050 is not equipped with front-wheel mudguards as are the other MFWD tractors.

New Styling Adopted Worldwide

On a cold January 29, 1989, this used 4450-MFWD, Serial No. 6,366, is seen in Darold Sindt's yard, Deere dealer at Keystone, Iowa.

Over 60 years' progress in tractor design is represented in this photo of an 8650 with an early Model "D" in the background in North Dakota.

A used 4240, Serial No. 14,356, with Power Shift transmission standing alongside a new 4850-MFWD outside Ron Schott's Sigourney, Iowa, dealership on January 27, 1989.

Largest tractor built to date by Deere, the 8850 was the only agricultural model fitted with a V-8 Deere engine, and it had 304 hp at the PTO. The photo shows an 8850 pulling a 915 V-ripper with nine standards. They were available with up to 13 standards for lighter land.

New Styling Adopted Worldwide

For orchard and vineyard work the 50-horsepower 2255 model came between the 2150 and 2350 in power. For orchard work the tractor was equipped with 18.4-16.1 rear tires while for vineyard work it was equipped with 14.9-24. Fronts were similarly 27-9.5-15 and 6.50-16, respectively. Other special models were the 2750 Hi-Clearance or Mudder, and the 2150, 2350, and 2550 could be optionally equipped low, narrow, or wide, and with slow (special creeper) gears.

Other Additions to 50 Series

In 1984 two further Yanmar-built models were added to the line, the 1450 with 51 horsepower and the 62-horsepower 1650, both with 4-cylinder engines. The latter achieved the distinction of being the most economical tractor tested at Nebraska to that time.

A specially designed model with offset driving position, reminiscent of the 2-cylinder Models "L" and "LA," the 900 HC was introduced in 1986 for certain row-crop work requiring precise control. It was aimed at growers of tobacco, strawberries, and other nursery plants. It had a 3-cylinder 25-horsepower Yanmar-built engine, 540-rpm PTO, 3-point hitch and an 8-speed transmission.

The first John Deere tractor equipped with MFWD as standard was the 3150, announced in 1985; its front-wheel drive engaged automatically when a high drawbar load demanded it.

The various options available for the model 2750 were extended in 1986 with the introduction of a low-profile model offered with either 2- or 4-wheel drive.

❶ This double mower-conditioner outfit is the ideal job for a 2550-MFWD.

❷ A lineup of new 2750 Mudder (High-Clearance) tractors outside a California dealer's premises on September 26, 1986.

❸ Showing its versatile nature, Gene Walker of Nichols, Iowa, has equipped his 2950-MFWD with a 260 front loader and 709 rotary cutter on September 17, 1989.

Ideal mates, the 1650, economy record holder at Nebraska, has an easy job baling hay with the smaller size 430 round baler.

This specialist 900HC is equipped with mid-mounted cultivator and 250S fertilizer and grain spreader.

The 95-hp John Deere 3150 has an automatic mechanical-front-wheel-drive system which engages when sensors detect engine exhaust temperatures approaching normal operating range.

129

New Styling Adopted Worldwide

New 55 Series for 1987 and 150th Anniversary

Despite the difficult economic conditions on American farms in 1987, the company introduced a new line of tractors, the 55 series, from 45 to 85 horsepower, built in the Mannheim factory. All models could have MFWD as an alternative to the standard 2-wheel drive, and there were five transmission options depending on model and particular requirements.

In addition to the five standard models there were two sizes of orchard and vineyard models built low and narrow, the 2355N and 2855N. During 1987 the 2155 and 2355 were offered as utility tractors for grounds care or highway use.

The 3- and 4-cylinder GP models, painted in all-yellow trim, had more transmission options than the standard tractors and could be ordered specification by specification, giving the purchaser more say over what extras he wished to choose. In 1988 the under-100-horsepower 55 series was completed with the introduction of the 3155-MFWD, replacing the 3150-MFWD. The Long Green Line was indeed getting longer.

The smallest of the 55 series models built in Mannheim, this 2155 fitted with shell fenders is tidying up a pasture with a 503 rotary cutter.

Fitted with simple ROPS and flat-top fenders, this 2355 has the new style exhaust pipe with curved top making a raincap unnecessary.

Seen at the first EXPO in Waterloo, the agricultural 2555-MFWD and highway 2755-MFWD make an interesting comparison. Both have the earlier exhaust and raincap, but the former has flat-top fenders while the latter has shell type and a ROPS canopy.

Note the low and narrow nature of this 2855N as it pulls a sprayer in an orchard.

In the new tractor line at the second EXPO near Waterloo airport, this 2755 High-Clearance or Mudder tractor is the smaller 4-cylinder-engined option of this type which was available in 1990. The Mudder could also be purchased as the 6-cylinder 2955.

In latest standard U.S. market trim, a 6-cylinder 2955 is shown outside Goodrich Equipment Co. in Geneseo, Illinois, on September 23, 1989.

New Styling Adopted Worldwide

Palm Springs New Product Announcement Largest Ever

The author was privileged to be present at Palm Springs for the largest-ever new-product announcement in January 1989. Waterloo joined the earlier Mannheim series by announcing its 55 series. Instead of the five models of the 50 series, an extra model, the 4555, was added as the smallest of the wide-frame tractors.

Again the power of some models was uprated. In the narrower frame models, the 4055 was increased to 105 horsepower. The 4255 and 4455 remained at 120 and 140 horsepower, respectively. All models had turbocharged and completely redesigned engines, including the new 4555, which was rated at 155 horsepower; the 4650 and 4850 replacements, the 4755 and 4955, were increased to 175 and 200 horsepower, both having aftercooling. The 4955 was thus the first row-crop tractor with 200 PTO horsepower.

The new line included new automatic engagement of the MFWD, a new IntelliTrak monitoring system, new lighting and cab comfort features, and the three larger models electrohydraulic hitch control. The Hi-Crop 4255 replaced the similar 4250.

Dignity and impudence—a new 3155-MFWD dwarfs a beautifully restored 110 garden tractor, Serial No. 2,991, fitted with the original 7-hp Kohler engine, later increased to 8 hp. The 110 was the first model of the very successful lawn and garden products line now marketed worldwide by the company.

New 4055 and 4255 tractors with twin rears at the largest-ever new-product presentation at Palm Springs, California, on January 17, 1989.

A 4455, Serial No. 1,005, with twin rears is seen in the pavilion at the Palm Springs dealer and press presentation.

General view of the inside of SG2 cab fitted to 55 series tractors showing the clear deck and swivel seat.

Two-wheel-drive version of the 4555, the extra model introduced with the 55 series, seen outside Deere's Training Center in Davenport, Iowa, on August 9, 1990.

New Styling Adopted Worldwide

All-New 60 Series Articulated Tractors

In the fall of 1988 dealers had been called to the presentation at Denver of an all-new line of articulated 6-cylinder 4WD tractors—the 8560, 8760, and 8960.

They were completely new in design and concept, featuring new engines, a longer wheelbase, center-frame oscillation, and a redesigned Sound-Gard cab. This had a side-access door allowing a one-piece front screen with much improved vision, since, in addition, the muffler and airstack were moved to the right front corner of the cab.

There was an option of three transmissions: 12-speed Synchro, 24-speed Powr-Sync with built-in Hi-Lo, and 12-speed Power Shift. The 7.6-liter engine in the 8560 was rated at 235 horsepower, giving 200 horsepower at the PTO; the 10.1-liter 300-horsepower 8760 gave 256 PTO horsepower and the largest model had a Cummins 14-liter 370-horsepower engine, the company having abandoned its V-8 engine. The 8960 had 322 horsepower at the PTO. For the first time the company offered triple tires for greater flotation on the two larger models, with cast-center drive wheels and steel-center dual wheels.

This new 4755-MFWD, Serial No. 1,716, dwarfs a restored 6-speed "BN" owned by B. Chester of Morton-le-Moor, Yorkshire, at the Tractor Centennial Show organized by the Yorkshire Museum at Merton, England, on June 17, 1989.

The 4955 is the first John Deere row-crop tractor rated at 200 PTO hp. The 55 series have several new features including "auto" caster-action MFWD, IntelliTrak electronics, improved Sound-Gard body with increased visibility, and a new 7.6-liter engine.

Another photo taken at the Palm Springs new-product announcement showing 8560, Serial No. 1,007, and 8760, Serial No. 1,020. The 60 series articulated models were shown to dealers the previous fall in Denver.

The most powerful of the 60 series tractors was the 370-engine-hp 8960, seen here pulling a V-ripper.

New Styling Adopted Worldwide

Under-40-Horsepower Line Extended in 1989

The hydrostatic-drive compact tractors, originally introduced in 1986 with the 655, 755, and 855 models and built largely for the grounds care products market, was augmented in 1989 by the 33-engine-horsepower 955 which has MFWD as standard. The 655 was dropped from the line in 1990.

For the customer who required a gear-driven tractor the new 70 series built by Yanmar was announced in 1989. The five new models range from the 18.5-engine-horsepower 670 to the 38.5-horsepower 1070, replacing the 650-1050 with an additional 1.5 to 4 horsepower. All the related John Deere implements were interchangeable among the three 50, 55, and 70 series.

During 1991 the 95-horsepower 3155-MFWD was replaced with two new models, the 3055 with a naturally-aspirated 92-horsepower engine and 2-wheel drive only, and the 100-horsepower 3255-MFWD with 4-wheel drive as standard and a turbocharged 6-cylinder engine, extending to seven the Task Master models available from Mannheim (see photo in chapter 1).

This studio photo of the 1989 version of the hydrostatic-drive 955 shows it in the original style of that series.

The 20-hp 755, 24-hp 855, and 33-hp 955 were restyled in 1992 to allow an increase in cooling capacity from 3.8 to 4.5 liters. Three cab options were available in Europe; the Mauser KK955 model shown rates 82 dB(A) at the operator's ear. The 955 is standard with MFWD; the 755 and 855 are optional 2- or 4-WD.

Making an interesting comparison with the photo of the 955, this 16-PTO-hp 670 is the smallest of the 70 series gear-driven tractors.

A 30-PTO-hp 970 equipped with mid-mounted mower deck, ROPS, and vertical exhaust, the latter two options are more common in farming applications.

Proving its agricultural parentage, this MFWD-equipped 70 series tractor with 80 loader brings home the hay bales.

New Styling Adopted Worldwide

Largest 155- to 200-Horsepower Tractors Fine-Tuned to Become 60 Series

For the 1992 season the three largest Waterloo models became the 4560, 4760, and 4960 but retained all the basic features and engine power of the 55 series models they replaced.

By shifting the muffler to the right-front corner of the Sound-Gard body and moving the air intake to below the hood enabled the cab to be redesigned to give a cleaner forward view and much easier access.

Augusta Works Built for 5000 Series Production

The first three of a completely new series of 3-cylinder tractors, built in a brand new factory in Augusta, Georgia, were announced in 1992. The 40-horsepower 5200, 50-horsepower 5300, and 60-horsepower turbocharged 5400 represent a totally new design concept with access from either side facilitated by console-mounted controls and a lower, further-forward operator position. This was made possible by moving the fuel tank to a position behind the seat.

Servicing is simplified by a tilt-up hood, and side panels that are removable without recourse to tools. The ROPS is foldable and MFWD is optional, while hydrostatic power steering is standard on all models. The PTO is the 540-rpm independent type, and the transmission has 9 forward and 3 reverse speeds. A multitude of new and existing mounted (Category 2/1) and drawn equipment is available for use with these new-styled units.

This studio photo of a 2-wheel-drive 4960 clearly illustrates the new position of the exhaust muffler.

A 5200 in an English setting; the only 5000 series tractor in the United Kingdom at the time of writing, Serial No. 220,927, was imported by John Dorrell of Pershore, Worcestershire, from Canada. It fills a specific farming requirement in the Vale of Evesham better than any alternative make or model.

The three large 60 series tractors have a number of improvements over the 55 series they replaced. The muffler is moved to the cab corner and the air intake is under hood. Improved steps and access deck, with batteries below, make entering the cab much easier. The tractors now carry a 5-year, 5,000-hour warranty.

A 60-hp 5400 is posed with a 40-hp 5200 and a 50-hp 5300 MFWD fitted with a new 540 front loader. All of these tractors have the preproduction decals, which have now been changed to the style shown in the opposite photo.

New Styling Adopted Worldwide

An All-New Breed of Power

6000 4-Cylinder and 7000 6-Cylinder Models for 1993

The fall of 1992 saw the most revolutionary development in John Deere tractor models since the New Generation multi-cylinder series replaced the 2-cylinder line in 1960. Announced in both the States and Europe simultaneously, the new 6000 series 4-cylinder and 7000 series 6-cylinder models have few parts common to the series they replace.

The all-new modular design means that the power, comfort, hydraulics, and steering are all new, resulting in new productivity and performance. The one item which allows this total rethink in tractor design is the use of a heavy-gauge, independent steel mainframe.

A longer wheelbase and the moving of the fuel tank to below the operators platform permits the new ComfortGard cab (known as the TechCenter cab in Europe) to be set further forward, so that the operator sits ahead of the back axle. At the same time it also allows access from both sides, a desired feature lacking in the earlier Sound-Gard body.

With glass from floor to roof, and the muffler now at the corner of the cab as on the 60 and 70 series articulated tractors, the visibility provided is virtually 360 degrees. This, plus the reduced noise level to 72 dB(A), the combined adjustment of steering wheel and command module, and the automotive-type ventilation, and air-quality system, means that the new cab answers everyone's requirements.

A rural setting is used for this photo of a 6300-MFWD with the European version of the new cab, named the TechCenter, with lighting to conform to Europe's standards.

The lowest powered of the 6000 series models on the U.S. market, this 6200 is the open-station 2-wheel-drive version with ROPS. Note the vertical exhaust and new-style fenders with this model. It makes an interesting comparison with the previous photo.

The three new 4-cylinder 6000 series tractors marketed in the States: the 2-wheel-drive 6200, 6300-MFWD, and 6400-MFWD, all fitted with ComfortGard cabs. Options include left exhaust as shown on the 6200 and 6300, or the cornerpost fitting of the 6400. The latter also has front-wheel guards, standard in Europe on tractors with 25-mph (40-km/h) transmissions.

The local dealer checks with the operator of this 7600-MFWD before it goes chisel plowing. A 6000 series 2-wheel-drive model attends to yard duties.

141

New Styling Adopted Worldwide

In the States the 6000 series has four new transmission options, a PowrQuad 16/12-speed or 12/12 with creeper option, and a SynchroPlus 12/4 or the same with a 9-speed creeper option between 0.14 and 0.88 mph. In Europe there are two extra PowrQuad options giving 20/16 or 24/16 speeds.

The larger models' PowrQuad transmissions have 16/12 speeds as standard in the States, with a 12-speed creeper option; in Europe the similar choice is between 16/12 or 20/12 PowrQuad without the creeper option.

In both zones the 7000 series have a new 19/7-speed Power Shift option giving clutchless shifting from 0.9 to 22.8 mph (40 km/h). When shifting from neutral to 19th gear the transmission goes straight to 11th gear and then one gear at a time automatically as a safety measure.

New 70 Series 4WD Tractors For 1993

Retaining the new styling adopted for the articulated 60 series models in this power class, the new 70 series were introduced in 1993 as the Power-Plus tractors. The previous models are increased in engine power from 235 to 250 horsepower on the 8570; the 8770 retains the 8760's 300 horsepower; a new model, the 8870, uses an uprated 10.1-liter engine giving 350 horsepower; and the largest model, the 8970, is the first John Deere tractor to break the 400-horsepower mark. All four models are equipped with new Electronic Engine Control.

The three larger models can be equipped with triple tires if required, and have the choice of three transmissions. The 12-speed Power Shift is not offered on the 8570. Independent 1,000-rpm PTO is an option on all four

In the wide-open country for which it was designed, this 300-hp 8770 on twin wheels all around is making rapid progress with a gang of four drills.

A 7-furrow reversible plow represents a good load for this 7800-MFWD tractor.

Cross-section of a 70 series showing the drive lines necessary to achieve articulation.

For the first time with the 70 series Deere made triple wheels on both axles an option, as on this 8870.

143

New Styling Adopted Worldwide

models, and the closed-center, pressure-compensated hydraulic system also applies across the line.

The two larger models have both front- and rear-wheel brakes. A new and exclusive feature is the Field Cruise Control, allowing the operator to set engine speed below the governed 2,100-rpm for consistent speed in planting or other light tillage operations.

New 6-Cylinder Models from Waterloo and Mannheim

The 7000 series was extended during 1993 with the addition of two standard models, the 92-horsepower 7200 and the 100-horsepower 7400. Both tractors have turbocharged 2,100-rpm engines, the former with 5.9 liter (359 cu. in.) capacity, the latter 6.8 liter (414 cu. in.) as in the 7600.

Both models are also available in Hi-Crop and High-Clearance format and all four models can be ordered with either 2WD (standard) or MFWD. The standard transmission on all four is a new 12-speed SyncroPlus unit with 16-speed PowrQuad optional and with 12-speed creeper an added alternative, as with the larger models. The 19-speed Power Shift is not available on these smaller tractors.

The Mannheim-built Models 2955, 3055, and 3255 have been replaced in the States by the two new Waterloo tractors. The new Mannheim-built 6-cylinder 6600 and 6800, being of similar power to the 7200 and 7400, were not required for the North American market.

They were duly announced in the fall of 1993. The 6600 and 6800 have MFWD as standard and are otherwise 6-cylinder versions of the 6400. PowrQuad transmissions are standard, 20/16 or 24/16 on the 6600, 16/12 or 20/12 on the 6800.

The high-clearance models are available in 6300 and 6400 sizes as open-station or with ComfortGard cab; nine additional creeper speeds give 13 ft/min to 19 mph with the 12-speed SyncroPlus and 12 added creeper speeds with the 16-speed PowrQuad transmission.

This side view of a 2-wheel-drive open-station model with ROPS, seen here drilling with a 750 No-Till drill, gives quite a different impression of the new 1993 7200 tractor.

A very good view of the 26.2-in. front-axle, 40.4-in. rear-axle clearance of one of the new 7200 Hi-Crop models.

The open-station 7200 Hi-Crop and 7400 High-Clearance model with cab are pictured in a hilly location; they joined the line in 1993.

Overseas Beginnings — Germany/France

The European Inheritance

Following the withdrawal from the Scottish scheme in 1951 the direction of the Deere & Company's overseas development was finally decided by the purchase in 1956 of the very old Lanz company in Germany with its factories in Mannheim and Zweibrucken. With this acquisition came an involvement in the associated company of Lanz Iberica in Spain and its works at Getafe near Madrid.

Lanz had been producing tractors since 1911, even earlier than Waterloo, and in 1921 it took a major step with the introduction of the first 12-horsepower crude-oil model or "Bulldog." A number of these original models have survived with collectors and museums; two or three are in the company's archives, one in Moline and at least two in Mannheim.

Over the next 37 years these diesel and semi-diesel Bulldog tractors were developed into a useful and powerful line of mostly standard-tread models, always retaining their simple single-cylinder design, with one exception—the D1666 fitted with an MWM 2-cylinder engine.

They progressed from the original concept to evaporative- or hopper-cooled models, followed by a radiator-cooling system and eventually the semi-diesels, some of which were in production when Deere took over the company.

Produced first in 1923, the Felddank had a 2-cylinder vertical benzine engine with 190- × 220-mm bore and stroke, governed to 650 rpm, giving 38 hp (28 kW).

Built from 1921-1926, the original 12-hp Bulldog-type HL crude-oil tractor had a similar 190- × 220-mm stroke and bore for its single cylinder 6-L engine but was governed at 420 rpm.

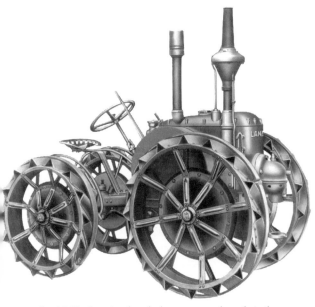

In 1923 the 4-wheel-drive articulated Acker-Bauern Bulldog HP model was added to the line and 722 were built between 1923 and 1926. This model had 15 hp, achieved by increasing the governed speed to 500 rpm.

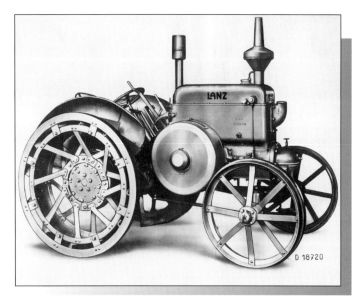

The first major improvement to the Bulldog line came in 1926 with the introduction of the HR2 Gross-Bulldog 22-28 hp model; the first production line in Germany was installed in the Mannheim factory in 1925-26 to build it. Its hopper-cooled engine was increased to 10 L (225 × 260 mm) with 540 rpm, giving 28 hp. It remained in production until 1931. As with the earlier models, reverse was achieved by reversing the engine.

The row-crop Bulldog was not popular in Germany. A John Deere "GPWT" served as the model for the HN1 in 1931. As row-crop attachments were not available in Europe only a few prototypes were built and Lanz did not proceed with its production.

The radiator-cooled standard-type tractors were popular; 25,000 HN2, HN3, and HN4 and over 40,000 HR5, HR7, and HR8 were built between 1929 and 1941. This 12-20 HN2, owned by Eric Barker of Wyverstone, Suffolk, was chosen to represent the small-radiator HN (D7500) series.

Overseas Beginnings — Germany/France

The production line of Model HR tractors in the Mannheim works.

This 45-hp 6-speed HR8 (D9506), Serial No. 133,255, belongs to Mr. Baker of Hailsham in England and makes an interesting comparison with a Field Marshal at the annual Dorset Steam Fair, the largest vintage show in Europe, on September 3, 1993. Note the left-side drive to the fan on these models.

The HE model D4506 or Farmer's Bulldog was produced in 1940. Only 276 were built before the government ordered production stopped. It was the first of a line of 15-hp 6-speed tractors for the small or row-crop farmer, and was revived in 1952 as the Model 5506.

The 17-hp D1706, produced from 1952-1955, was the first of a new series of semi-diesel tractors introduced in 1952. It is shown here with HR5, Serial No. 82,293, and HR8, Serial No. 650,680, owned by Tony Fisher, at the Peterborough Vintage Club's open day at Thorney in England on May 16, 1993.

Fitted with an 11-hp air-cooled engine, this D1106 Bulli tractor with its single-bottom mounted plow is in the John Deere Archives' possession in Moline. It was one of the smallest Lanz tractors built in the four decades covering this most successful line of tractors.

Lanz's second attempt at a twin-front-wheel row-crop model, the 28-hp D2803, was available in this form as well as the standard 4-wheel D2806 model. It too was a semi-diesel, there was also the 22-hp D2206.

The only production 2-cylinder diesel Bulldog built by Lanz was the Model D1666 fitted with a Motoren Werke Mannheim (MWM) 16-hp engine. It had 85- × 110-mm bore and stroke and was governed at 2,000 rpm. A similar motor was fitted in the A1806 Alldog tool carrier.

149

Overseas Beginnings — Germany/France

Final 1-Cylinder Designs Adopt the Green and Yellow

From 1958 the Bulldog models retained in production were painted in the company's green and yellow, and in due course carried the John Deere-LANZ name plates as well. Eleven models remained in the line: the 16-PS D1616, 20-PS D2016, 24-PS D2416 and 28-PS D2816 semi-diesels with the HE engine and 6-speed gearbox; the full-diesel 50-PS 6-speed D5006 and 9-speed D5016, 60-PS 6-speed D6006, 9-speed D6016 and 30-km/h D6017 for road work; and the last two models designed, the 40-PS D4016 and the baby of the line, the 12-PS D1206.

Built over the same period as the D1666 (1955-1960), the D1616 was fitted with a Lanz 16-hp single-cylinder full-diesel engine. This example is plowing a deep furrow with its 2-way plow.

Eric Barker of Wyverstone, Suffolk, owns this very tidy D4016, Serial No. 345,967, seen in its home farmyard. The 40-hp D4016 was the last Bulldog design to go into production in 1957, the year after Deere purchased the German company. It has a full diesel engine.

The second full-diesel model announced in 1955 was the D2016 20-hp tractor. This example, Serial No. 280,819, complete with the usual mid-mounted mower, was built in 1956, but could have been one of the first Lanz tractors painted green and yellow experimentally. It was seen at the first U.K. EXPO held at Wood Green, Huntingdon, on June 25-26, 1992; it is owned by Jim Thomas of Wokingham, Berkshire.

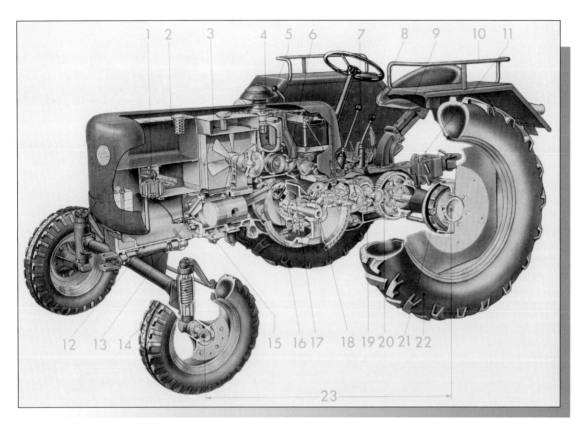

Cross-section of full-diesel Models D1616, D2016, D2416, and D2816.

The D6000 series was one of the last Bulldogs to be replaced by the multi-cylinder models. Introduced in 1954, the 6-speed 60-hp semi-diesel D6006, 9-speed D6016, and 30-km/h D6007 were the largest single-cylinder Lanz tractors built in Mannheim

Built narrow and low, the D2402 24-hp Bulldog, with similar specifications to the D2416, was introduced in 1956 for work in vineyards.

151

Overseas Beginnings — Germany/France

Europe's New Generation Models

The last single-cylinder tractors from Mannheim were built in 1960, and it was in January of that year, some eight months before the New Generation announcement in Dallas, that the first multi-cylinder models appeared from Mannheim works.

These were the 4-cylinder 28-PS model 300 and 36-PS 500 fitted with 1010 diesel engines from Dubuque, rubber mounted, with 10-speed forward/3-reverse Lanz gearboxes, and a sprung front axle. They carried Dreyfuss styling and had nameplates with John Deere-LANZ, emphasizing the latter name initially, as it was so well known in Europe. They replaced three of the Lanz single-cylinder models, the D2016, D2416, and D2816.

During 1962 two further models were introduced. The 2-cylinder 6F/1R-speed 18-PS 100 had side panels covering the engine compartment like the two larger models; it replaced the D1206 and D1616. The 50-PS 700, replacing the D5006 and D5016, was equipped with a Lanz 10-speed transmission similar to the original two models, but with a 2010 engine; it had no engine side panels.

All four new models had both 540- and 1,000-rpm rear PTO and 1,000-rpm mid PTO, plus independent hydraulics, with automatic load and depth control for both Category 1 and 2.

The largest single-cylinder 60-PS Lanz 6000 series tractors were replaced by 55-PTO-horsepower 3010 models imported from the United States.

In France Deere joined the French consortium of Compagnie Continentale de Motoculture or CCM in 1959. From 1965 the tractors built by this company in Saran, the 303, 303V, and 505, carried the John Deere-CCM emblem.

The prototype models for the new John Deere-LANZ tractors were tested in Germany, Holland, Italy, and the United States. The illustration shows an early design suggestion for a 18-hp (LX-D) single-cylinder tractor, which was never put into production.

The 300 and 500 tractor assembly line in the Mannheim factory.

Preproduction models were shipped by air to Waterloo for testing at the John Deere Engineering Center. They were sheeted in the road container to avoid identification. This illustration shows the pre-100 (LX-F) 2-cylinder model in early guise before the Dreyfuss styling was finalized (as shown in chapter 1).

A 500 with 3-bottom mounted plow at work in Germany in 1960.

The 18-hp 2-cylinder 100 was introduced in 1961, a year after the 28-hp 300 and 36-hp 500, for the many small farmers in Europe.

Largest of the four new John Deere-LANZ models was the 50-hp model 700 seen here plowing in Germany.

153

Overseas Beginnings — Germany/France

First New Generation European Models Updated

For the French and Spanish markets the mid-size models were redesigned with Standard-Triumph and Perkins 4-cylinder engines, respectively, shell fenders, and without engine side screens, as on the 700. The engine in the 303 gave 37 horsepower, while the 505 gave 44 horsepower.

In 1966 the three larger Mannheim models were upgraded to the 10 series and given the new 20 series engines from Dubuque; the following year the 100 was replaced by the longer-stroke 2-cylinder 25-PS 200, retaining 6 forward gears, but now with 2 reverse. New larger models were the 32-PS 310, 40-PS 510, and 50-PS 710. The latter was the only model of this series exported to the U.K.

The Lanz name was retained on the German market for obvious reasons, although now smaller on the nameplate (same size as the owning company) but for other markets it was dropped, as it had already been on the French-assembled 303 and 505.

Some of the trademarks used in the early days of merger with various overseas companies: 1) John Deere-Lanz; 2) CCM—a French co-operative formed by Rousseau, Remy, and Thiebaud companies; 3) CCM-John Deere, used later; 4) Chamberlain (Australia); 5) JD John Deere (Argentina).

This standard 37-hp 303 has downswept exhaust, shell fenders, adjustable front axle, and pan seat with cushion.

The 44-hp 505 had the same specifications as the 303, and they both retained the 10/3 transmission and 540- and 1,000-rpm PTO of the earlier Mannheim models.

Handling three bottoms with ease, this 510 is busy plowing in Canada.

Retaining its John Deere-LANZ nameplates, this 710 is working down a seedbed in Germany.

Standing outside the works in Mannheim, the new 200 for the German market retains the John Deere-LANZ nameplates, while the 710s in the background for export have only John Deere on theirs.

Overseas Beginnings — Germany/France

A World Tractor Design

Because of the interim 10 series, and although announced in the States in 1965, the new 20 series "World Design" tractors were not introduced in Europe until 1967. At a stroke the various problems of the earlier series were overcome and Deere dealers had a fine tractor to sell.

Initially there were five sizes and eight models announced: the 3-cylinder models 34-PS 820, 40-PS 920, and the 47-PS 1020 in standard, orchard, and vineyard modes, and the 52-PS 1120; the 4-cylinder model was the 64-PS 2020 in either standard or orchard trim. In 1968 the 4-cylinder turbocharged 72-PS 2120 was added to the line and in 1969 the 86-PS 3120, the first 6-cylinder model to appear from the Mannheim factory.

In September 1967 the first five models of the new 20 series were displayed for the press: 820, 920, 1020, 1120, and 2020.

The 1020 was available as an orchard model or in narrower form for vineyard work as shown here, when it was designated 1020-VU.

A 3-cylinder 40-PS 920 busy at work plowing with a 2-furrow integral 2-way plow.

156

A studio photo showing the 1120 with European-style fenders and 4-post ROPS, removable toolbox position, and usual lights and trafficators.

This 2020 has the optional vertical air intake, full European-style fenders, and is plowing with a 3-bottom integral plow. There would appear to be little chance of wheelslip.

This 3120 has a man-size job pulling the very popular F145 semi-integral plow, the usual mate of a 4020.

Overseas Beginnings — Germany/France

30 Series Retains 20 Series Styling

In 1972 the three largest Mannheim models were uprated and became the 71-horsepower 2030, 79-horsepower 2130, and 97-horsepower 3130. They retained the styling of the previous series, the smaller 820, 920, 1020, and 1120 models continuing in production.

The new models had newly designed engines with larger bore, larger oil pump, and an alternator in place of a generator. The transmission and rear axles were strengthened to match the increase in horsepower.

The following year an extra model, the 59-horsepower 3-cylinder 1630, was added to the line giving five 3-cylinder models, two 4-cylinder, and the single 6-cylinder 3130. The new model retained the earlier styling in its standard, orchard, and vineyard form.

During this transition period several outside firms built cabs for these tractors, the most popular were Fritzmeier in Europe and Duncan in Scotland. The Sound-Gard body on the Waterloo models set the standard, and Mannheim accepted the challenge with the introduction in 1974 of the OPU or Operator's Protection Unit for the 2130 and 3130. At the same time the U.S. Power Front-Wheel drive was offered as an option on these two models.

The clean lines of the first 1030 tractors are well illustrated on this one with full fenders and 4-post ROPs.

A 71-hp 2030 with vertical exhaust and ROPS is hauling manure in Turkey.

158

On a misty day in Wales a 2-wheel-drive 2130, Serial No. 153,297, in its working clothes and fitted with a Scottish-built Duncan cab awaits the auctioneer's hammer.

A 2130 fitted with hydraulic Power Front-Wheel Drive and OPU makes an interesting comparison with the previous photo.

A 3130-PFWD equipped like the previous 2130 is plowing with a 2-way plow.

Overseas Beginnings — Germany/France

Mannheim Follows Waterloo's New Style

It was three more years before the whole Mannheim line was re-styled to match that adopted by Waterloo in 1972. With the new style in 1975 the whole line, including the three smaller tractors destined for Europe and Canada, continued as the 30 series and retained the same model numbers. One exception was the 2030 exported to Canada, which became the 1830 to avoid confusion with the 2030 Dubuque model.

Another 6-cylinder model was introduced in 1978, the 3030 with 86-DIN-horsepower filling the power gap between the 2130 and 3130.

Three further new models were introduced for users with high-clearance requirements. They were the 1030M, 1630M, and 2030M or multi-crop models destined to be continued in the various series up to today, and built in the Getafe factory.

Smallest of the new-style 30 series, this 830 has vertical exhaust, a European-designed 4-post ROPS, and canopy. It is pulling drawn disks.

The 1030 is equipped with a John Deere 58 front loader; note the resulting revised position of the toolbox.

A 1630 with front fenders plowing somewhere in Germany.

A field view of a 2130 equipped with shell fenders as supplied to the Canadian market in place of the more typical full type fitted in Europe.

This Mannheim-built 3130 has trafficators fitted by the nose of the tractor for easier viewing by oncoming traffic.

An early studio picture of a 4230 fitted with hydraulic PFWD and the initial extra lights and turning indicators required under local law.

Overseas Beginnings — Germany/France

40 Series

The tractors built in Mannheim for the U.S. market became the 40 series in 1975 with a new numbering range, but it was late in 1979 before the European 40 series was announced, coinciding with the introduction of the 50 series in the States. The two markets were often out of step in the numbering of their current series.

These new models were introduced as New Profiles of Performance. This was literally true, the profile of the hood rising toward the instrument panel to enable the fitting in due course of the Sound-Gard cab, but more of that shortly. In the meantime the OPU was modified to take this change.

All models from the 1040 up were now available with this cab option, and from the 940 up with a mechanical front-wheel drive made by an outside supplier, an option which was popular much earlier in Europe than in the States. The lack of braking effect had mitigated against the U.S.-built hydraulically operated PFWD.

With the opening of the new factory in Bruchsal near Mannheim, a new cab, the SG2, was produced for the 1640 up in 1981. The OPU was continued for the 1040 and 1140 in low-profile form.

At the same time three models were uprated, the 2040S, 4040S, and 4240S having about 5 extra horsepower each. For the 1983 season the original MFWD was replaced with a unit having a center driveline and an exclusive 12-degree caster angle or tilt through the pivot axis on the steering knuckle, allowing a 50-degree steering angle.

The 50-hp 1040 was available as a highway tractor, when it was painted industrial yellow. This particular model is the L-P series low-price version fitted with a low-profile OPU cab allowing the tractor to pass through low doors.

❶ Right-side view of the new 34-hp 840 with 4-post ROPS and canopy.

❷ A 44-hp 1040 with OPU cab and the early offset-drive MFWD is plowing in pleasant countryside.

❸ The agricultural version of the L-P series models is illustrated here in 56-hp 1140 guise, with a low-profile OPU cab. The emphasis during the difficult economic conditions of 1985 was on top value at low price.

The 2040 was uprated in 1981 from 70 hp to 75 hp and renamed the 2040S. The 4040 and 4240 were similarly treated. This model has the open 4-post ROPS version of the SG2 cab and optional air-intake extension and dust bowl.

This 8-year-old 1640 fitted with SG2 Sound-Gard cab is seen outside the John Deere dealer's premises in Devizes, England.

163

Overseas Beginnings — Germany/France

To cope with difficult economic conditions on Europe's farms, two new sub-series were introduced for the 1984 season, the X-E low-priced but fully equipped tractors, and the L-P low-profile models with a low cab line for livestock farmers.

The same year saw the introduction of a third 6-cylinder model, the 3640, with 112 DIN horsepower, MFWD as standard, and a front 3-point hitch and PTO option. This enabled the farmer to double, or even triple, the jobs which could be performed in one trip across the field.

In March 1986 a second cab option for the 1040 through 2040S models was announced—the MC1 low-profile and low-cost version of the OPU.

Fitted with special wheels and Terra tires giving low ground pressure, this 2-wheel-drive 2140 is spraying a winter grain crop in November 1988.

On April 30, 1993, a well-kept 3040-MFWD, equipped with the later center-driven MFWD, poses in front of a newly arrived 6400-MFWD in Devizes, England.

An immaculate used 2-wheel-drive 3140 has the new 3350-MFWD and 3050-MFWD tractors in the background at a Gloucestershire dealer's yard on May 18, 1990.

A 3140-MFWD, Serial No. 390,215, photographed on a damp and misty Welsh farm. The OPU cab makes an interesting comparison with the Sound-Gard body on the 2-wheel-drive model.

Overseas Beginnings — Germany/France

Large Tractors from Waterloo

The full 40 series Waterloo line was shipped to Mannheim and partly assembled there for distribution in Europe, plus the extra S models already mentioned.

Anticipating the introduction the following year of the 50 series from Mannheim, the 140-PS 4350 was introduced to replace the 4240S for the 1986 season.

Two photos which again offer an interesting comparison. The 4240S has MFWD, new style front weights and light position, and the muffler is behind the air stack.

At a farm dispersal sale near Faringdon in Berkshire, England 4040, Serial No. 300,389, awaits the auctioneer's presence on March 30, 1993.

The 4440-PFWD, plowing deep on August 13, 1992, in Suffolk, England, has the earlier front weights and light position, and the muffler is ahead of the air stack.

A PFWD-fitted 4040 with SG2 cab plowing a wide sweep with a reversible plow.

Owned by Robert Self, a well-known contractor and vintage tractor collector near Ipswich, England, this 8640 is fully occupied with a large U.K.-built reversible or 2-way plow.

Overseas Beginnings — Germany/France

50 Series

The big news in the overseas markets for 1987 was the announcement of the 50 series from Mannheim, still in production at time of writing up to the largest 4-cylinder model, the 2850. The opportunity was taken with this series to introduce a new model numbering system, with the 3-cylinder 1350 through 1850, the 4-cylinder 2250 to 2850 and the three 6-cylinder models 3050, 3350, and 3650, the latter with MFWD as standard. The 65-engine-horsepower 3-cylinder 1950 was added the following year.

The 1350 was offered with a safety frame only, the other 3-cylinder models had the option of it or the MC1 cab, while the 4-cylinder tractors added the SG2 cab option. The 6-cylinder tractors were offered with SG2 in standard or low-roof style for use in low buildings. Open-station tractors could be purchased with rollover protection and a sun roof option. Front 3-point hitch and PTO were available on the 2250 and larger models.

The third new cab produced in Bruchsal was the CC2 for the 3- and 4-cylinder models. Announced in December 1990, it had doors on both sides, a clear deck with the shifting levers console mounted, tiltable steering column for easy access, and a deluxe upholstered seat, giving the smaller tractors large-tractor comfort.

Lined up outside Frank Sutton's premises (a John Deere dealer in Raglan), the 1750 and 2350 are joined by an 855 on April 27, 1989. This Welsh dealer has other locations for the Consumer Products line.

On May 31, 1989, this 1850-MFWD with new-type curved-top exhaust and MC1 cab is seen at the Mannheim Works display area adjoining their museum.

A 1550-2WD tractor fitted with a new MC1 cab and integral sprayer is seen at work in Germany. Note the original straight-type exhaust with rain cap.

A 2-wheel-drive 2250 with front-wheel guards and SG2 cab heads for home under the famous Rhine bridge at Nijmegen on May 26, 1989.

With downswept exhaust and MC1 cab, this 1950-MFWD finds the 3-bottom reversible Mustang plow an easy load in light soil conditions.

Since it is increasingly difficult to find tractors with 2-wheel drive to photograph, this 2450, with a 300 series conventional baler, makes a pleasant change as it bales straw.

Overseas Beginnings — Germany/France

With old-type exhaust but with front PTO and hitch, an SG2-equipped 2650-MFWD demonstrates the height of tip of the attached trailer.

The SG2-equipped 2850-MFWD was seen on September 8, 1990, at the Yesterday's Farming Show in Somerset with a new 545 round baler and 955 Zweibrucken-built combine as backdrop.

The last 3650 built in Mannheim, Serial No. 775,621, was delivered in February 1994 to Lampeter Agricultural Services, Deere dealer in Pembrokeshire, southwest Wales. Robin Saunders, dealer principal, on the left, is joined by Jack Jenkins, his sales manager with 26 years' service; Shan Evans and Rachel Pearce, receptionists; Simon Norris, Tom Kirkham and Chris James, service dept.; and Steve Lawton, parts manager.

An unusual find in a barn at North Oakley on October 2, 1993, this 3050 with SG2 cab has 2-wheel drive and front-wheel guards.

Unloading maize, as corn is called in Europe, this 3350-MFWD is serving one of the new Z-series combines from Zweibrucken, a Model 2058 with row-crop head.

Smallest of the Waterloo-built 50 series tractors, this 4050-MFWD still dwarfs the onetime largest model built there, "R," Serial No. 14,055, on May 11, 1990.

171

Overseas Beginnings — Germany/France

Mannheim Joins World "Revolution"

Mannheim's part in the 1992 "New Generation" of tractors was the production of the 4-cylinder 6000 series. Four models were available in Europe—the 75-engine-horsepower 6100, 84-horsepower 6200, 90-horsepower 6300, and 100-horsepower 6400. For the U.S. market, only the three larger were exported.

As is the usual practice, the new models were extensively tested on selected farms. The first Waterloo 7000 series tractor to come to Europe, a 7800, camouflaged under the model number it was to replace, the 4455, worked on a Yorkshire farm in 1991.

With the new design, the tractors were much lighter per horsepower available, so that greater loads could be carried, a significant gain with the increasing use of front, as well as rear, 3-point hitches and PTOs.

First of the 6000 series tractors seen by the author, this 6100 with MFWD and TechCenter cab, as the Comfort Cab is known in Europe, is pictured at the Girvan, Scotland, dealer's premises on October 6, 1992.

A 6200-MFWD arrived on the loading bay at the Devizes dealership in England on April 30, 1993.

OECD-Test Reveal

A World Record For John Deere

OECD Test No. 1427*
200 g/kWh
at max. engine power

OECD Test No. 1427 showed that the 6400 was the fuel efficiency champion in the 100-hp class, requiring only 200 g/kWh at maximum power.

Straight from work, this 6400 2-wheel-drive tractor, Serial No. 108,387, is on a farm near Salisbury, England, on January 17, 1994.

Overseas Beginnings — Germany/France

Six-Cylinder Mannheim Models Added in 1993

For the 1993 season the 3- and 4-cylinder 50 series models with CC2 cabs remained available as did the 3350 and 3650 6-cylinder SG2 tractors.

Late in 1993 the 6-cylinder 110-horsepower 6600 and 120-horsepower 6800 were added to the line. As described in chapter 1, the new models soon proved their worth. Demand by the farming community was such that the biggest problem for the company's dealers was again one of delivery.

This 110-hp 6600-MFWD is making the most of its 25 mph (40 km/h) top transport speed.

The extra length of the 6-cylinder tractor's hood is demonstrated in this photo of the first 6800, Serial No. 118,092, in the U.K.—the one shown at the Royal Smithfield Show in December 1993, and seen at the Wilton, Wiltshire, Deere dealership on January 17, 1994.

The cab on one of the new 6800 6-cylinder models shown tilted in this studio picture.

Overseas Beginnings — Germany/France

When supplied for use on roadways, models of the 6000 series available in Europe are painted highway orange. A number of attachments are available: front loader, road sweeper blade, rear backhoe, spreader, and hydraulic linkage mower. 2WD and MFWD are optional.

The interior of the TechCenter cab shows the spacious accommodations and the ease of access through both doors.

The first 7000 series tractor to come to Europe, a 7800, is seen in suitable "camouflage," of the model it replaced, on the Smith family farm at Withcall, near Louth, Lincolnshire, in September 1991 (from left: son, Drew; father, Henry; and son, Martyn).

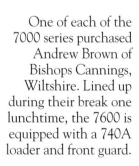

One of each of the 7000 series purchased Andrew Brown of Bishops Cannings, Wiltshire. Lined up during their break one lunchtime, the 7600 is equipped with a 740A loader and front guard.

177

Further Overseas Developments: Spain, Italy, and Mexico

Spain Joins the Deere Fold

The Getafe factory of Lanz Iberica started building the single-cylinder Bulldog tractors the year Deere acquired the parent company, and so continued doing so until 1963. Seven models were made, with 28, 36, 38, 40, 60, and 65 horsepower, plus a compact 30-horsepower narrow version for use in Spanish vineyards and orchards.

In 1956 the semi-diesel 36-horsepower D3606 was the first model built in Getafe; this was followed in July of that year by the 38-horsepower D3806. In October 1959, the much larger 60-horsepower D6006, and in February 1960, the newly styled 28-horsepower D3016, joined the expanding line. By June the 38-horsepower D3850 replaced the older-style D3806, and in 1961 a low and narrow vineyard model, the 30-horsepower D3012, was added.

The last of the single-cylinder tractors to be built in Getafe was the full diesel 40-horsepower D4090 and the largest of all, the 65-horsepower semi-diesel D6516. In addition, hay rakes, cultivators, other tillage tools, and farm trailers completed the line.

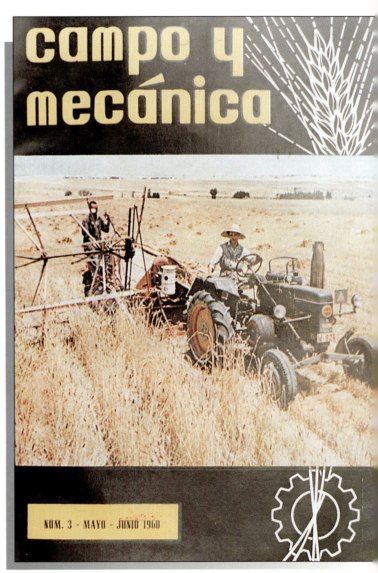

The front cover of the Spanish Furrow, *Campo y Mecanica*, for May-June 1960, showed one of the original D3606 semi-diesel Getafe-built Bulldogs cutting a crop of grain with a Lanz binder.

An early photo of the original Lanz Iberica Bulldog assembly line in the Getafe factory near Madrid, Spain.

In the last Lanz color scheme of blue and orange, this English-language sales leaflet shows the 30-hp D3012 Getafe-built vineyard model.

A similar model to that in the next picture, a D4090 is seen outside the works at Getafe.

This ghost image of the new 40-hp D4090 reveals the clean lines achieved in the last of the Bulldogs.

Further Overseas Developments: Spain, Italy, and Mexico

Deere's First Spanish Model

The association with John Deere resulted in the investment of several hundred million pesetas in the machinery and tooling for a new tractor, the 505. It was introduced at the first dealer convention in Spain in 1963, and was the first Deere-designed tractor to be built in Getafe.

Three years later the 10 series line of four models followed: the 515, 717, 818, and a compact version of the smallest model, the 515V. The latter were designed for the ubiquitous Spanish vineyards and orchards.

The first John Deere designed tractor to be built in Getafe was the 505, derived from the Mannheim 500, but fitted with a Perkins 4-cylinder 44-hp engine. The placing of the John Deere logo on the hood was not pursued after this initial attempt.

Largest and most powerful of the three new 10-series models, which replaced the 505 in 1966, the 60-hp 818 is plowing three furrows in a typical Spanish setting.

The 56-hp 717 was the Spanish equivalent of the German-built 710 and is shown here with a mid-mounted mower.

Illustrating the very narrow style of the vineyard models, this 45-hp 515V is working among the trees.

Further Overseas Developments: Spain, Italy, and Mexico

Spain Announces 20 Series

The 20 series was introduced in 1969 even though it had already been in production in Dubuque for three years and for two years in Mannheim. The world tractor design had found more new outlets.

The 1020, 1520, 2020, 2120, and 3120 were produced. Again the emphasis in the Getafe-built tractors was on the specialist vineyard and orchard models, a trend which continues at the time of writing. The vineyard model and two orchard models were the 1020VU, 1020OU, and 2020OU, respectively.

This 1520, with four cylinders and 52 hp, in standard trim has full fenders, vertical exhaust and air intake, and the first type of wrap-around front weight. Note too the traffic indicators below the headlights.

Designed to work in narrow spaces, the 3-cylinder 1020VU with the same 45 hp rating as the 515V it replaced is working among the vines (above) and the fruit bushes (below).

A 4-cylinder 61-hp 2020 with 30 forage harvester is working on a Spanish farm.

Another typical Spanish setting for a 72-hp 2120, baling straw with a 214 pick-up baler built in Arc-les-Grays, France.

Further Overseas Developments: Spain, Italy, and Mexico

Getafe's 30 Series Announced

In 1973 the 30 series was introduced in Spain, still using the original 20 series styling. Spain's identification for the models it produced was now established; S for standard models, VU for vineyard, EF for orchard, and M for multi-purpose or high-crop. The specialist models included the two vineyard 1030VU and 1630VU; three orchard 1030EF, 1630EF, and 2030EF; and three high-crop, 1030M, 1630M, and 2030M.

These model classifications were later refined to S-2 for 2-wheel drive, S-4 for 4-wheel, V for Vineyard and F for orchard (fruteros).

The larger of the two vineyard models, this 3-cylinder 57-hp 1630VU outside the Getafe works shows its compact design. Note the front drawbar with cover fitted, protruding through the front weight.

Largest of the orchard models, the 68-hp 2030EF is working among the trees.

The three Spanish orchard models take a photocall: from left 1030EF and 1630EF, both 3-cylinder, and the 4-cylinder 2030EF.

An unusual combination of vertical air intake and downswept exhaust is shown in this photo of a standard 2030 plowing.

This 6-cylinder 90-hp 3130 is in standard trim and is plowing stubble with a reversible plow.

Further Overseas Developments: Spain, Italy, and Mexico

35 Series Has New Styling

Peculiar to Spanish-speaking markets, a 35 series was introduced in 1977, adopting the new styling used on the later 30 series elsewhere in Europe. Vineyard models of the 1035 and 1635, orchard models 1035, 1635, and 2035, and multi-purpose models 1635 and 2035 were produced in Getafe.

The 2035 was the only 35 series model with a hydrostatic front-wheel drive option, and was available from 1977 to 1979. The 35 series had engines of the same power as the 30 series they replaced.

A studio picture of one of the smaller 1977 35 series tractors. This 1035 has downswept exhaust and the usual European-style full fenders.

Orchard version of the 1035, with downswept exhaust and shell fenders, at work among the trees.

A studio view of the next larger size model, the 1635, again with downswept exhaust but with full fenders.

This right-side studio view of the 2035 with vertical muffler is part of a Getafe photo set.

A nice view of a 75-hp 4-cylinder 2135 at work with a 4-furrow integral plow; note the new-style front weights.

The 3135 6-cylinder 90-hp model gives a good impression of power in this last photo of the 35 series set.

187

Further Overseas Developments: Spain, Italy, and Mexico

Spanish "Schedule Masters"

The 40 series or "Schedule Masters" launched in 1980 offered farmers new levels of safety, comfort, and increased productivity with the introduction of the 4-post Roll-Gard, SG2 cab, and center line-drive MFWD options.

Two extra-size models were introduced with this series, the 72-horsepower 1840 and the 110-horsepower 3340, both available in S-2 or S-4 (MFWD) mode.

The original intention was to build the 3640 in Getafe; a prototype with local cab was built but cost considerations resulted in the model being imported from Mannheim.

With the new styling including recessed headlights for the vineyard models, the 3-cylinder 50-hp 1040V has a more streamlined look.

Studio photo of the 1140F orchard model with downswept exhaust.

The 1140-S4, as the model was designated in Spain when equipped with MFWD, is plowing with a 2-furrow reversible plow and has a 4-post ROPS.

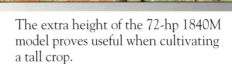

The extra height of the 72-hp 1840M model proves useful when cultivating a tall crop.

Another view of a vineyard tractor at work. The front weight used as a front drawbar can be seen on this 56-hp 3-cylinder 1140V model.

Further Overseas Developments: Spain, Italy, and Mexico

A SG2 Sound-Gard air-conditioned cab makes working in the noonday sun tolerable for an operator of this 2040 S-2 4-cylinder 70-hp tractor.

This 2040 S-DT with 12-degree caster-action MFWD has an SG2 cab to complete its specifications, relatively deluxe by Spanish standards.

This studio photo gives a good impression of the OPU cab fitted to a 4-cylinder turbocharged 2140 S-4, as supplied in Europe before the SG2 Sound-Gard cabs were available.

An open-station 6-cylinder 3140 S-2 with shell fenders, pictured in the studio.

Showing the 12-degree caster-action and axle details of the new MFWD, this 3340 S-4 is pictured in a field setting.

The 3640, shown in a wintry setting, has U.S.-style flat-top fenders and Roll-Gard ROPS with canopy. It also has the earlier-style rearward-sloping hood and larger muffler.

Further Overseas Developments: Spain, Italy, and Mexico

50 Series Introduced and Line Lengthened in 1987

With the introduction in 1987 of the 50 series, a proliferation of sizes appeared, numbered similarly to the Mannheim tractors. There were three 3-cylinder, four 4-cylinder, and two 6-cylinder tractors. They were the 1750 (vineyard only), 1850, and 1950 3-cylinder; 2250 (added in 1993 in place of the 1950), 2450, 2650, and 2850 4-cylinder; and 3150 and 3350 6-cylinder.

Current styles include standard (S), orchard (F), vineyard (V), and multi-crop or high-crop (M). In France the orchard models are called the 1950N and 2650N and have different fenders and light positions. The first three styles have MFWD (double-traction or DT in Spain) as an option.

The 3650-MFWD was imported from Germany for a time. Production ceased on the 3-cylinder 1950 in 1992, and on the 3150 and 3350 at the end of 1993. The rest of the 3- and 4-cylinder models up to the 2850 were still in production at the end of 1993, but the probability is that Getafe will become a components factory in the near future.

The highest point on the 1750V illustrated is the rear-view mirror. The position of the headlights gives it an unusual appearance.

The advantages of the extra clearance of the 1850M are obvious in this photo of one spraying vines.

The 1850F is ideally suited to the many orchards found in Spain and elsewhere.

The various 1950 model options are shown in the next three photos. This photo of a French 1950N shows the different fenders and light position compared with the 1850F in the previous photo.

Two examples of the standard 1950S-2, seen at Getafe on April 5, 1989. They show the earlier and later (1989 on) exhausts; the curved top of the latter obviated the need for an exhaust rain cap.

Two 1950s seen at Getafe are the standard model with MFWD and 4-post ROPS and an orchard model behind. Larger fenders plus vertical exhaust and air intake are features of the former, and the latter orchard version has its own distinguishing style of fenders.

Further Overseas Developments: Spain, Italy, and Mexico

A Time of Change

Many of the Spanish-built tractors are sold as open station models due to local weather conditions and the type of farming, but the cabs produced in Bruchsal are optional on models other than the specialist types.

With the introduction of the 4-cylinder 6000 series in Mannheim in 1992, followed by the 6-cylinder models in 1993, the larger 50 series tractors were dropped from the Getafe line.

For the 1993/94 season the 6100-6400 4-cylinder and the 6600 and 6800 6-cylinder models are imported from Mannheim and have been sold to date with the TechCenter cab; for 1994 the 4-cylinder models will be offered with the open station option, and this could doubtless apply to the 6600 in the future. The 7600-7800 models come from Waterloo and all have cabs.

From Augusta the 670 compact tractor fills a niche in the Spanish market.

Getafe continues to supply standard, vineyard, orchard, and high-crop models of the 50 series up to the 2850. There were eight standard models from the 1850 to 3350, all with MFWD option; two sizes of vineyard, the 1750SV and 1850S; and four orchard models, 1850SF, 1950SF, 2450SF, and 2650SF both SV and SF styles available with either 2WD or MFWD; and four high-crops, the 1850SM, 2250M, 2450SM, and 2650SM, with 2-wheel drive only.

During the company's sesquicentennial, on March 10, 1987, the 150,000th tractor built in Getafe was exhibited at the works—a 4-cylinder 2450S-DT with Sound-Gard SG2 cab and both vertical exhaust and air intake.

The MFWD of this 2650SF-DT helps in orchard work on steep terrain.

Making full use of both its front and rear linkage, the operator of this 2850 S-DT has the luxury of air-conditioning to ease his workload. The 2850 is the largest model built in Spain at the end of the period covered by this book.

This photo illustrates the cranked front axle and drop rear axles used to obtain the necessary high clearance required with these models.

This 6300 is the open-station 4-wheel-drive version with simple ROPS. Note the vertical exhaust option and new-style fenders on this model.

Further Overseas Developments: Spain, Italy, and Mexico

Italian Models Adopted for Small European Farms

At the same time the 50 series was introduced in Spain, arrangements were made with Goldoni to market some of their small tractors for orchard use and even smaller units for very small farms and holdings.

For the former, the 42-engine-horsepower 445, 49-engine-horsepower 604, and 60-engine-horsepower 614 were the first models marketed. All of these models had MFWD as standard equipment. They were soon replaced by four models, the 42-horsepower 1445, 48-horsepower 1745, 56-horsepower 1845, and 67-horsepower 2345.

The smaller models introduced included the rigid-frame 4-equal-wheel-drive 933RS-DT, 938RS-DT, 1038 and 1042. Articulated models included the 921, 933, and U-238; the last two digits of all these seven models indicate the engine horsepower.

Smaller even than these machines were 2-wheel models 49I, 59LD, 140, and 719 for terrace working.

For 1993-94 the 4-equal-wheel Italian-built line is simplified to one rigid model, the 1042, and two more and larger articulated, the EURO 42 and EURO 50. The special small tractors built by Goldoni still include the 921, 933, and U-238 articulated-frame models, and the larger 1745FA, 1845FA, and 2345FA orchard tractors. The 42-horsepower 1445 orchard model was no longer listed for the Spanish market.

196

The largest of the first Goldoni models was the 60-hp 614. It was identical in appearance to the 604 but had a 105-mm-bore engine, giving it 60 engine horsepower.

The 38-hp 2-cylinder U-238 is a middle-size articulated model with four equal-size wheels.

❶ The first three models from Goldoni are lined up in this photo. The 445, 604, and 614 set the style standard for all subsequent models built to date by the Italian firm.

❷ The 49-hp 604 was fitted with a 3-cylinder 100- × 105-mm engine running at 2,600 rpm. In addition to its low overall height, with an 8-forward/4-reverse transmission and MFWD especially suited it to orchard work. The example shown has the early model identification decal.

❸ Smaller of the new articulated models with four-equal-size 18-in. wheels, the EURO 42AW is one of the latest of these Goldoni tractors in the line.

Replacing the 614, the 67-hp 3-cylinder turbocharged 2345 was available originally as an orchard tractor in both Europe and the United Kingdom. The Spanish market continues to import the Goldoni models for the 1994 season.

Further Overseas Developments: Spain, Italy, and Mexico

Mexico Assembles Waterloo and Mannheim Tractors

After importing the 620 and 720 2-cylinder tractors from the States through their branch house, Industrias John Deere S.A. de C.V. started to assemble the 435, 630, 730, and 830 models in Mexico, followed by the New Generation 3010 and 4010 tractors in the early 1960s. These were followed in turn by the 3020 and 4020 in 1964.

Europe supplied engine and transmission assemblies for the 1020 and 2020 in 1966 and the 2120 in 1971. A minimum local content of 60% was required by the Mexican government to allow manufacture there. The 1020 was available in its three styles, LU, RU, and HU, while the 2020 was offered as RU, HU, and an industrial version.

The 35 series was introduced in 1973 with the 4435 and followed the next year by the 4235, both based on Waterloo models. In 1975 the 2535 (illustrated on page 212 of Volume 2 of *John Deere Tractors and Equipment*) and the 2735 replaced the 20 series models.

A basic Mexican 2735 with flat-top fenders planting corn.

A 4435 Turbo at work with a 3751 Mexican-built 3-disk plow.

This 4-cylinder 72-hp 2555 is in Mexico. The flat-top fenders in the 55 series have a single light on each side.

The first 2755 models were equipped with a Perkins engine, as in this example shown. The headlights were mounted European-style in the front grille, an interim measure before adopting the Saltillo style of placing one light under each fender.

The lowest powered of the six 2755 models still in production at the time of this writing, this naturally aspirated model with John Deere 4-cylinder engine has 64 hp at the PTO.

Further Overseas Developments: Spain, Italy, and Mexico

55 Series Built in Saltillo

Having purchased the former IH factory in Saltillo, Deere built a new 55 series there from 1983. Two versions of the 72-horsepower 2555, a standard and an orchard model, and four of the turbocharged 82-horsepower 2755 covered the local market requirements. These latter included standard, orchard, and Hi-Crop models, the first two available with MFWD.

In the larger tractor field the 4235 and 4435 were replaced by the 140-horsepower 4255 and 153-horsepower 4455 in 1983-84. Deere had now become the largest manufacturer of tractors in Mexico.

When fitted with the turbocharged version of the 239-cu.in-engine, the 2755T has 69 PTO hp.

This Mexican open-station 4455 2-wheel-drive tractor has twin rears and 4-post Roll-Gard ROPS and is disking.

The 2755 Turbo Synchron is equipped with a Top Shaft Synchronized (TSS) transmission and has 75 PTO hp.

An example of the later models produced in Mexico, this 2755 Turbo tractor has MFWD, called "doble traccion" or double traction in Mexico, and the new-style full fenders and lights, although still fitted with a vertical exhaust with rain cap.

Unlike the rest of the 2755 series, the orchard (huertero) model has shell fenders and the earlier-style headlights within the front grille.

Photo taken by Roy Harrington of a 2-wheel-drive 4255 outside a Mexican dealer's premises, with twin rear wheels and Mexican-type fenders.

The 2755T Hi-Crop (Alto Despeje) model is similar to the 50 and 55 series Mudders of the United States; the Mexican models are chiefly used in horticultural areas. The one shown has the new-style curved exhaust designed to eliminate the need for the weather flap previously used.

Southern Hemisphere: Argentina, South Africa, and Australia

Argentina's 2-Cylinder Models

Argentina was more significant to Deere than the Mexican market. The British company Agar Cross, based in Buenos Aires, had been the agent for South America for the company since the end of the last century. It introduced the Model "D" as soon as it was available to the export market. In 1929 alone 2,194 John Deere tractors were sold. Argentina was Deere's largest export market.

In 1957 the board authorized the construction of the Rosario plant to assemble tractors locally. The following year the 730 was produced with a percentage of local content. Four styles were adopted: standard, row-crop with twin front wheels or wide front, and Hi-Crop.

In 1963 the 445, the Argentine version of the U.S. 435, was added and five types were produced: RU regular, RU deluxe, T tricycle row-crop, O orchard, and V vineyard.

One of the later 730 Hi-Crop models with the all-green hood side panels and industrial-type John Deere nameplates.

▼ This 730 diesel row-crop model with wide front is painted in the original U.S. style with yellow hood side panels but with the Argentine medallion used to avoid trademark infringement. The tractor is cutting grass with a 16 rotary chopper.

All the 445 models lined up at the works in Rosario. From the left, 445T tricycle, 445RCU row-crop utility with oversize tires and shell fenders, 445 RCU economy version with smaller tires and no fenders, 445V vineyard model, and 445-O orchard model.

The deluxe version of the 445RCW is seen working with integral disks.

With a mounted caster-wheel mower, this 445 RCU is the economy model without fenders and with small front tires.

Southern Hemisphere: Argentina, South Africa, and Australia

20 and 30 Series Built in Rosario

In 1970 these models gave way to the 20 series: 1420, 2420, 3420, and 4420. These were followed in 1975 by the 30 series: 1030, 2330, 2530, 2730, 3530, and 4530, all but the last being local versions of Mannheim models. In 1977 another 4-cylinder model, the 3330, was added to the Rosario line, plus two more 6-cylinder models, the 4730 and 4930, which were imported from the States.

This field view of the 3-cylinder 52-hp 2330 is the Argentinian equivalent of the Mannheim 1130, and has downswept exhaust and adjustable rear axles.

Group photo of the 20 series tractors built in Rosario between 1970 and 1975. In front, the 3-cylinder 43-hp 1420 with 3-furrow integral plow, next the 4-cylinder 2420 66-hp with planter, and two 6-cylinder models, the 77-hp 3420 with 6-furrow semi-mounted plow and the largest model, the 102-hp 4420 with 7-furrow drawn plow. All models have shell-type fenders and front headlights, and the three larger favor Waterloo styling although equipped with Saran engines. All have adjustable front and rear axles.

❶ Painted in industrial colors, the studio study shown of the 727 open-station model was the Argentinian equivalent of the 3020 Classic tractor from Waterloo.

❷ Studio photo of the 2330-V vineyard model. The swept-back front axle allowed very short turns, and the downswept exhaust and low headlight position offered protection for branches.

❸ This 4-cylinder 2530 has vertical exhaust, shell fenders, and adjustable rear axles.

The 4-cylinder 74-hp 2730 was introduced in 1975. Note the rear fenders, a similar style to that used in Mexico—an interesting comparison with the 2530.

Southern Hemisphere: Argentina, South Africa, and Australia

40 Series Arrive in 1981

When the 40 series arrived in Argentina in 1981, Deere had increased its tractor market share from 14% to 29.3% or nearly a third. The other major manufacturer competition was Deutz, Fiat, and Massey-Ferguson. The new line included the 1140, 2040, 2140, 3140, and 3540 of German design (the latter three models built in Rosario from 1983), and the 4040 from the United States.

The 4-cylinder 3330 introduced in 1977 used the same engine as the 2730 but had an 8-speed forward, 2-reverse Syncro-Range transmission in place of the 8-forward, 4-reverse of the latter. The new model was altogether larger than the similar-powered 2730.

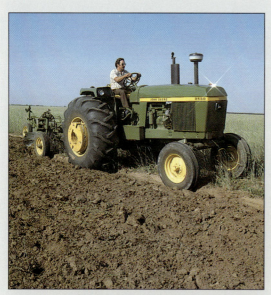

An open-station 3530 in typical Argentine format, with flat-top fenders, is plowing.

Largest of the 30 series models imported into Argentina was the 4930, the equivalent of the 4630 in the States. Seen here with a 4-post ROPS, it had a 6-cylinder turbocharged and intercooled engine.

With a 7-furrow semi-integral plow, this Argentine 4530, built between 1975 and 1980, has a full workload.

For farmers requiring a small low-profile tractor the 1140 was ideal.

The turbocharged 4-cylinder 2140 introduced in 1983 was a popular mid-size tractor, and remained in production in Rosario until 1988.

Southern Hemisphere: Argentina, South Africa, and Australia

Last Rosario Models Still in Production

The 4040 was replaced in 1984 for two years by the 4050, but it was 1988 before the rest of the models were changed to the 50 series. By then the number of basic models built in Rosario was reduced to three: the 2850, 3350, and 3550. The 2850 was offered in 2-wheel-drive format, the 3350 with both 2-wheel or MFWD, and the 3550 with MFWD as standard. These three models remained in production to the end of the period covered by this book. The 4450-MFWD was imported from Waterloo until it was replaced by the new 7000 series.

Shown in industrial yellow in Volume 2 of *John Deere Tractors and Equipment*, the 121-hp agricultural equivalent of the 3540 is seen here with MFWD and without cab or ROPS, the most usual specification in Argentina.

In 1988 it was decided to reduce the number of models built in Rosario to three. The smallest was the replacement for the 2140, the 2850, with 95-hp 4-cylinder turbocharged engine, seen here disk plowing.

In 4-wheel-drive form the model was called the 3350 DT for double traction.

The middle size of the three models from Rosario was the 3350, available with either 2- or 4-wheel drive. The 6-cylinder normally aspirated engine of this tractor produced 110 hp.

Largest of the three models introduced in 1988 was the 3550, only offered with MFWD and fitted with a 125-hp 6-cylinder turbocharged engine. It is seen here with a locally built hydraulically controlled drawn plow.

Southern Hemisphere: Argentina, South Africa, and Australia

Imported Models Extend the Argentine Line

In the fall of 1992 nine models were imported from the States to supplement the three 50 series built in Rosario. These were the 5400 (with either 2- or 4-wheel drive) from Augusta, and from Waterloo the 4760 DT and 4960 DT, the 4-wheel-drive articulated 8570, 8770, and 8870, and the new 7700 and 7800.

One of the first 2000 series tractors in John Deere green and yellow, this 2800-MFWD with Zetor deluxe safety cab is plowing with a 4-furrow reversible European-built plow.

Imported from Waterloo, the 4960-MFWD, shown here, and the 2-wheel-drive 4760 presently fill the top-of-the-bill spot in the market in Argentina.

Sent to Argentina from Augusta as complete units, the 5400 covers the lower end of the power scale pending the arrival of the 2000 series from the Czech Republic. Here is a 5400-MFWD equipped with a 540 front loader and bucket.

Also from Waterloo, the 125-PTO-hp 7700 and 145-PTO-hp 7800 fill the gap between the home-produced 3550 and the Waterloo 60 series. This 7700 is fully equipped with front hitch and PTO, front fenders and European-style trafficators and side lights.

The largest tractors imported into Argentina are the 70 series articulated 4-wheel-drive Models 8570, 8770, and 8870 from Waterloo. Shown is the most powerful of these, the 350-hp 8870.

211

Southern Hemisphere: Argentina, South Africa, and Australia

South Africa—Local 41 Series Introduced in 1982

Although Deere was assembling Mannheim tractors in the Nigel factory, which had opened in 1962, the South African government decided that from 1982 all tractor companies building tractors in that country must fit the locally built Perkins (Atlantis Diesel Engine Co. or ADE) engine.

It was estimated that Deere tractors required 175 parts to convert from the Saran-built engines used until then. Despite this, the operation proved profitable and by 1980 the company had reached 17% of the market, well up from the 4% of the early 1960s. This placed it fourth to Ford (22%), Massey-Ferguson (22%), and Fiat (20%), but only just...

The first series built in Nigel was the Mannheim 40 series, locally called the 41 series. This series had five sizes and 12 models: the 4-cylinder naturally aspirated 46-kW 1641 and 1641F orchard model, the altitude-compensated 57-kW 2141, turbocharged 63-kW 2541 and 71-kW 2941, and the 6-cylinder AC 3141, all available as standard 2-wheel-drive or optional MFWD, except for the orchard model.

51 Series Supersedes 41 Series in 1987

In 1987 the 51 series replaced these, and the number of models increased to 13 in six sizes. Smallest was the naturally aspirated 4-cylinder 2251 or 2251N in orchard/vineyard form with 2-wheel drive (TWD in South Africa) or MFWD; next the 4-cylinder 2351, 2651, and 2951T (turbocharged), and the 6-cylinder 3351, all four having TWD or MFWD option; and finally the 6-cylinder 3651 with MFWD only.

The 4-cylinder 1641F narrow-version orchard model was equipped with a naturally aspirated 46-kW 236 ADE engine built in South Africa.

Four of the standard model sizes of the 51 series originally produced in Nigel are shown here as a group for the front page of the 1988 sales brochure.

212

Largest of the 41 series models, the 3141 had a 6-cylinder altitude-compensated 354C ADE engine. It was available with either 2-wheel drive or Caster/Action MFWD.

All models except the 3651 could be purchased with 2- or 4-wheel drive. The 2351 and 2651 have 4-cylinder altitude-compensated ADE engines of 55 kW and 60 kW, respectively. The 3351 and 3651 6-cylinder tractors are also altitude compensated, giving 74 and 82 kW.

Southern Hemisphere: Argentina, South Africa, and Australia

The 2351, 2651, 3351, and 3651 models were all fitted with altitude-compensated engines, giving a greater intake of air on the Highveld. Mixing this extra air with fuel gives improved combustion, producing the same power one would obtain at sea level.

At the end of 1993 only the three smaller models, the 2251/2251N, 2351, and 2651 remain in production. The last of the Mannheim production of 3350 and 3650 6-cylinder tractors were imported, pending the results of South Africa's spring elections.

This 2651 has 2-wheel drive and was still in production at the end of 1993.

The 4-cylinder naturally aspirated 2251N is the smallest model in the 51 series. Its engine gives 46 kW and it is supplied for orchard and vineyard work.

The 3351 was one of the 6-cylinder models on which production was been stopped pending the results of the country's first multi-racial elections. Unlike the 3651, it was available with 2-wheel drive as well as MFWD. Its 354C altitude-compensated engine gave 74 kW, with 66 kW at the PTO.

This 3651-MFWD has a 2-post Roll-Gard ROPS with canopy, an option not always used in South Africa.

215

Southern Hemisphere: Argentina, South Africa, and Australia

Australia and Chamberlain in 1948

Bob Chamberlain of Chamberlain Industries Ltd conceived the idea of an Australian-built tractor in the late 1930s, and the firm built their first two prototype tractors after the war in 1948. These early models had 2-cylinder engines, but unlike the Johnny Poppers in the States they were horizontally opposed like the early Waterloo Boys.

The company's first attempt at a diesel model was in 1952 when the GM 3-cylinder 2-cycle 3-71 engine was fitted in the 60DA. Two years later the 55DA with Chamberlain's own 2-cylinder opposed diesel engine was announced. It was built until 1957.

One of the first Chamberlain 40K production tractors pulling a 7-furrow drawn plow at a demonstration in 1949. These first models had a 2-cylinder horizontally opposed all-fuel engine giving 40 engine, 36.3 belt, and 30.8 drawbar horsepower in Australian Tractor Test No. 1.

The first of the Chamberlain diesel tractors, the 60DA with a GM 3.71 3-cylinder engine, was introduced in 1952. This was followed in 1954 by the 70DA or Super 70. An earlier restoration is shown at Bendigo in March 1993.

Kerosene models were increased in power through the 40KA, 45K and KA, and 55K reaching their final development in the 55KA with 60 engine hp. The 55KA, as well as the 40K behind it, is owned and was restored by Greg Baker of Burdcup, Western Australia.

216

Close-up of the 40K 2-cylinder horizontally opposed engine—left side view.

Right side of same 40K engine.

The diesel version of this 2-cylinder tractor, the 55DA is at a show in Australia.

Southern Hemisphere: Argentina, South Africa, and Australia

First of the Champions

In 1955 the company decided to rely on Perkins 4- and 6-cylinder engines, and these were fitted to most models until 1975. The first model so fitted was the Champion 6G announced in 1955 with a Model L4 engine, followed two years later by the 9G with its later 4-270 replacement.

The opportunity was taken to introduce a new styling for the Champion series, thus getting away from the very "IH" look of the first models. The Super 70 was restyled at the same time and became the Super 90.

By 1958 the need for a larger tractor saw the introduction of the first Countryman Mark 1, initially fitted with a Meadows 4-330 diesel engine. Nearly 2,000 tractors, including the Countryman Mark 2 and 3, were built with this engine, before the Perkins 6-354 was adopted for the Countryman 6 in 1963.

With the market for large tractors covered, the need for a smaller one became apparent, so in 1959 the Crusader appeared with the 4-270 engine. However, only 216 units were built over four years, so this model was discontinued.

A more successful venture, introduced the same year, was the Canelander, which was the Champion fitted with adjustable axles for row-crop work. With the 4-cylinder engine it stayed in production until 1967; then the Perkins 6-cylinder 6-306 was fitted until 1972.

❶ The first of the long line of Champion models, the 6G was introduced in 1955 with new styling in place of the "IH look" of the first models. This model earned great fame in the Redex Round Australia Car Trial, acting as a backup and rescue vehicle. The 6G was fitted with a Perkins L4 diesel engine, and is shown with the cab as "Tailend Charlie," as the trial vehicle was known. It had added front and extended rear mudguards, special tires, and extra headlights.

❷ The 6G was replaced in 1958 with the 9G which had the later Perkins 4-270D engine.

❸ The Countryman 6, introduced in 1963, had the Perkins 6-354 engine. It retained the second Chamberlain style. Note the different exhaust position and larger air cleaner on this restored model from the one above.

The Countryman was introduced in 1958 to satisfy the demand for a larger tractor. The example shown, a Mark 3, was fitted with a Meadows 4-330 engine, as had been the Mark 1 and 2, and appeared at a vintage tractor rally in Australia.

The final requirement in the late 1950s was for a row-crop model; the original Canelander was a Champion 9G with adjustable front and rear axles.

The Crusader was announced in 1959 to cover the lower end of the power scale. It used the same Perkins 4-270D as in the Champion 9G and Canelander.

219

Southern Hemisphere: Argentina, South Africa, and Australia

Third Styling Exercise for 1966

For the 1966 season the Countryman 354 and Champion 306 were given more modern styling, not unlike Deere's early industrial models of the late 1950s and early 1960s.

The year 1970 saw the merger with Deere and the introduction of the C series tractors. The Countryman became the C6100 and the 6-cylinder Champion the C670, while the 4-cylinder version was the 236B, 236L and 236DB (for base, linkage and drawbar models). Thirty C456 tractors were built in 1972/74 with the Perkins 4-212 engine, and in their last year of production 50 of the 236 models were fitted with the John Deere 4-cylinder 239 engine.

When the Countryman 354 was announced in 1963 the opportunity was taken to again modernize the appearance of the tractors, resulting in the third pure-Chamberlain style. The Perkins 6-cylinder engine replaced the previous 4-cylinder Meadows engine.

The 306 was the first of the Champion series to be fitted with a 6-cylinder engine. Like the earlier 4-cylinder model, the Perkins engine was chosen, giving 70 hp at 2,000 rpm, 57.6 hp at the PTO, 57.4 drawbar hp, and 54.7 at the rear-mounted belt pulley (figures from Australian Tractor Test No. 52.).

The Champion 236 was offered in basic form, with linkage, or as a drawbar-only model. This linkage model is at the Welshpool Works in Western Australia. The Perkins-engined 236 was superseded for one year in 1975 by the 239 fitted with a John Deere 4-cylinder engine, but only 50 were built before the next major design change took place.

Final model of the Champion line, the C670 replaced the 306 and was fitted with the same Perkins 306 6-cylinder engine. Hydraulic 3-point linkage was optional to the standard drawbar. When tested at Werribee in February 1971 (A.T.T. 66), the C670 gave the same horsepower figures as the 306 except that the PTO had 58.7 hp.

A Countryman C6100, one of the last Chamberlain-designed models before the Deere influence became apparent, seen hard at work with a Chamberlain disk plow. Largest of the Chamberlain models, the C6100 in A.T.T. No. 72 gave 107 engine hp, 80 PTO hp, and 89 drawbar hp; it was not tested on the belt pulley. Test tires were front 11.00 × 16, rear 23.1 × 26.

221

Southern Hemisphere: Argentina, South Africa, and Australia

Deere Influence Shows in New Series

With Deere expertise now available in engineering and manufacturing, a new series of "Sedan 80" models were announced for 1975; in Australia the word Sedan indicates a fitted cab. With new looks and a smart yellow color scheme, the new tractors were an immediate success.

Announced in four sizes and five models, the line included the 68-PTO-horsepower 4-cylinder 3380, the 85-PTO-horsepower 4080 offered as a standard tractor or a cane-farming version with adjustable wheel tread and 6-post ROPS frame, the 98-PTO-horsepower 4280, and the turbocharged 119-PTO-horsepower 4480; all the last four had 6-cylinder 359-cubic-inch Deere engines.

All but the cane model had a new design of safety cab, incorporating a 6-post protective frame; it was the Australian equivalent of the European OPU. With these new tractors the company's share of the market rose to 21%, making it the largest agricultural tractor company in Australia.

For 1981 the original 80 "A" series was updated to the "B" series. All models of both series had on-the-go hydraulic Hi-Lo shift transmissions with 12 forward and 4 reverse speeds, full-length steel chassis, hydrostatic power steering, and mechanical differential lock.

Category 2 3-point linkage was standard on the 3380 and optional on the 4080 and 4280 of both series. "Live" PTO with built-in, multi-disk clutch and band-type brake, both hydraulically engaged, was standard on all models. It disengaged automatically when the engine stopped, its brake was engaged when the engine was running, and it could not be turned by hand when the engine was stopped, giving 3-way safety.

At another rally in Australia, this beautifully restored 85-PTO-hp 4080 standard tractor, with 6-cylinder Saran-built engine and Sedan safety cab with air conditioning and heating, looks as good as new.

A different angle on this twin-rear-wheeled 4280, which has 98 hp at the PTO and a 12-speed-forward, 4-speed-reverse Hi-Lo transmission.

- Centrifugal air spin dust ejection precleaner.
- John Deere–built diesel engine featuring high torque reserve.
- Large capacity fuel tank, forward mounted for better weight distribution.
- Quartz halogen headlights for improved visibility.
- Full length steel chassis.
- On-the-go hydraulic Hi-Lo shift.
- Constant mesh collar shift transmission.
- Easy to service swing-out batteries.
- Inboard planetary reduction final drives.
- Heavy duty differential.
- Cat. II 3 point linkage with top link sensing (not available on 4480B).
- Deluxe seat, adjustable to height, weight and leg length.
- Hydrostatic power steering for easier, safer manoeuvrability.
- Air conditioned 6 post ROPS sedan body.

This cross-section of the 4280B is representative of the whole Sedan line.

The 4-cylinder 3380B and the 6-cylinder 4080B and 4480B were fitted with 3-point linkage as standard. The 4080B was offered with adjustable front and rear tread for cane farmers or in standard trim as shown here. The "B" series had minor design and styling changes.

The 119-PTO-hp 4480B was the largest and most powerful of the Sedan tractors built in Welshpool. Fitted with a 6-cylinder turbocharged 123-hp John Deere engine, it was only offered as a drawbar tractor but could have twin rear wheels as an option.

Southern Hemisphere: Argentina, South Africa, and Australia

The final models announced in 1985 were the 90 series, now painted in green and yellow, but still under the Chamberlain name. The four power sizes were the 94-horsepower 4090, 118-horsepower 4290, 137-horsepower 4490, and the 164-horsepower top-of-the-line 4690. The two smaller tractors had 359-cubic-inch engines, naturally aspirated in the 4090, turbocharged in the 4290, and the two larger models had turbocharged 466-cubic-inch engines. PTO horsepower at rated engine speed of the four models was 94, 110, 129, and 154, respectively.

The appearance and the internal layout of the new safety cab was even closer to the SG2 now supplied elsewhere. It had tinted safety glass, 310-degree field of vision and a 78.0 dB(A) sound level.

All models had adjustable rear-wheel tread, and 2-wheel-drive models could have an adjustable front axle as an option. Optional 3-point linkage was Category 2 on the two smaller models, Category 3 and 3N on the two larger. Caster/Action MFWD with its 13-degree angle was an option, for the first time in Australian-built tractors, on all four models.

In 1985, for the first time, the Chamberlain tractors were painted green and yellow and the new cabs had the Sound-Gard-type roof. All 90 series were powered by a high-torque 6-cylinder diesel engine, the three larger models being turbocharged. All could have either 2-wheel drive or 13-degree Caster/Action MFWD; all four 2WD models with linkage could have adjustable front axles.

A typical Australian scene with this 118-engine-hp 4290 drilling with a Chamberlain combine seeder. The cab's square lines compared with the Sound-Gard are apparent.

The interior of the new cab on the 90 series shows its family resemblance, if squarer style, to the Sound-Gard body built in both Germany and the United States.

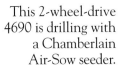

This 2-wheel-drive 4690 is drilling with a Chamberlain Air-Sow seeder.

The largest and most powerful tractor built in Welshpool was the 4690 with a 164-hp turbocharged and intercooled engine. It was equipped as standard with Category 3 and 3N linkage and 12/4-speed Hi-Lo transmission with a top speed of 25.8 mph (41.6 km/h). This 4690 has MFWD and twin rears; the 4490 is 2-wheel drive.

Southern Hemisphere: Argentina, South Africa, and Australia

Czech-Zetor

During 1993 Hans Becherer, company chairman, announced an agreement with the Czech firm of Zetor to market their line of eight 43- to 91-PTO-horsepower tractors as a lower-price product, initially for South America, the Far East, and other emerging markets.

Argentina was one of the first to announce their availability, which will market the 3-cylinder 2000, 4-cylinder naturally aspirated 2300, and turbocharged 2800. All eight models are offered with the choice of cab or open station, 2WD or MFWD, Category 2 toplink sensing, cerametallic dry clutch, and hydrostatic steering.

All have hydraulically operated disk brakes, wet-disk in the case of the three larger. Rear PTOs are dependent and independent 540-rpm as standard on the five smaller models, with independent 540/1,000 rpm optional; the three larger are fitted with independent 540/1,000-rpm as standard, operated pneumatically by hand lever.

The engines of the 2000, 2100, 2200, and 2300 are naturally aspirated; while the 2400, 2700, 2800, and 2900 are turbocharged. All eight are rated at 2,200 rpm.

Most powerful of the three larger models, the 106-engine-hp 2900 is similar in appearance to the other two, the 89-hp 2700 and the 100-hp 2800 which is to be marketed in Argentina. All 2000 series tractors can be purchased with or without cabs and as 2WD or with MFWD.

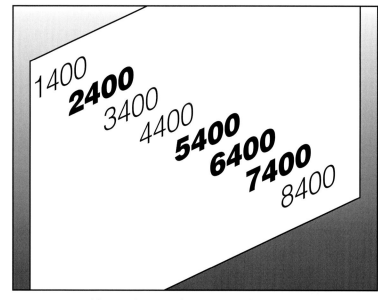

For 1994 and beyond... A 3/4000 series from the cooperation with Renault to replace the Mannheim 50 series? An 8000 series from Waterloo to replace the 60 series? We have to be patient and wait and see. Whatever Deere designers have in store, it is bound to be exciting for the users of the Green and Yellow...

Appendices

A-1 – Worldwide Tractor Comparisons
United States - European - Other Equivalents

U.S. Models			European Models				Other Models			
Year	PTO-hp	Cylinders	Year	Engine-PS	Cylinders	Variations & Notes	Year	Model	Cylinders	Country
			1960	300-28	4	Lanz 10-speed transmission	1963	303	4	France
1960	1010-36	4		500-36	4	Lanz 10-speed transmission		505	4	France/Spain
1960	2010-46	4	1962	700-50	4	Lanz 10-speed transmission				
				100-18	2	Lanz 10-speed transmission		445	2	Argentina
	3010-59	4		3010(Assembled EUR)		U.S. 8-speed transmission	1958	730	2	Argentina
1965	1020-38	3	1965	310-32	3	Lanz 10-speed transmission				
				510-40	3	Lanz 10-speed transmission	1966	515	3	Spain
				200-25	2	Lanz 10-speed transmission				
	2020-54	4		710-50	4	Lanz 10-speed transmission		717	4	Spain
1967			1967	1020-47	3	U.S. 8-speed transmission		818	4	Spain
	2020-54	4		2020-64	4	U.S. 8-speed transmission				
1968	820-31	3		820-34	3	U.S. 8-speed transmission				
				920-40	3	U.S. 8-speed transmission				
	1520-46	3		1120-52	3	U.S. 8-speed transmission	1970	1420	3	Argentina
1969			1968	2120-72	4	U.S. 8-speed transmission		2420	4	Argentina
			1969	3120-86	6	U.S. 12-speed transmission		3420	6	Argentina
								4420	6	Argentina
1972	4430-125	6					1973	4435	6T	Mexico
	4230-100	6					1974	4235	6	Mexico
(1st style)	2030-60	4	1972	2030-68	4		1973	2030	4	Spain 1st style
(30 series)				2130-75	4			2130	4	Spain 1st style
				3130-80	6			3130	6	Spain 1st style
1973	830-35	3						1030	3	Spain 1st style
	1530-45	3	1973	1630-56	3			1530	3	Spain 1st style
	2630-70	4		No equivalent				1630	3	Spain 1st style
							1975	2330	3	Argentina
								2530	4	Argentina
								2730	4	Argentina
			1975	3380-68	4	Australia	1976	3330	4	Argentina
				4080-85	6	Australia	1975	3530	6	Argentina
				4280-98	6	Australia		4530	6	Argentina
				4480-119	6T	Australia		4930	6	Argentina
			1975	830-35	3		1975	2535	4	Mexico
				930-41	3	2nd 30 series style (Europe)		2735	4	Mexico
1975	2040-40	3		1030-48	3		1977	1035	3	Spain 2nd style
(1st style)				1130-51	3					
(40 series)	2240-50	3		1630-56	3			1635	3	Spain 2nd style
	2440-60	4		1830-60	4	Canada		2035	4	Spain 2nd style
	2640-70	4		2130-75	4	Not equivalent to 2640		2135	4	Spain 2nd style
1977	2840-80	6		3130-92	6			3135	6	Spain 2nd style
			1978	3030-86	6					
1979			1979	840-38	3		1980			40 series Spain
2nd style)				940-44	3					
(40 series)	2040-40	3		1040-50	3					
	2240-50	3		1140-56	3					
				1640-62	4		1982	1641	4NA	South Africa
	2440-60	4		2040-70	4			2141	4AC	South Africa
				2040S-75	4T			2541	4T	South Africa
	2640-70	4		2140-82	4T			2941	4T	South Africa
	2940-81	6		3040-92	6			3141	6AC	South Africa
							1981	2140	4T	Argentina
				3140-100	6			3140	6	Argentina
1977	4040-90	6	1981	4040S-115	6T		1986	3540	6T	Argentina
	4240-110	6		4240S-132	6T					
1982	Waterloo 50 series					Introduced 1984 Europe	1985	40/42/44/4690		Australia
1983	2150-46	3				MFWD non-caster available	1983	2755NA	4	Mexico
	2350-56	4				MFWD caster available		2755T	4T	Mexico
	2550-66	4				MFWD caster available		2755TS	4T	Mexico
	2750-75	4T				MFWD caster available		2755F	4T	Mexico
	2950-85	6				MFWD caster available		2755HC	4T	Mexico
			1984	3640- 112	6	MFWD caster standard				
1985	3150-96	6				MFWD caster standard				

228

A-1 – Worldwide Tractor Comparisons (continued)

U.S. Models			European Models				Other Models			
Year	PTO-hp	Cylinders	Year	Engine-PS	Cylinders	Variations & Notes	Year	Model	Cylinders	Country
1986			1986	4350-140	6T	MFWD caster available				
				1350-38	3	MFWD caster available				
	2150-46	3		1550-44	3	MFWD caster available				
				1750-50	3	MFWD caster available				
				1850-56	3	MFWD caster available				
	2350-56	4		2250-62	4	MFWD, Front hitch/PTO extra	1987	2251	4NA	South Africa
	2550-66	4		2450-70	4	MFWD, Front hitch/PTO extra		2351	4AC	South Africa
	2750-75	4T		2650-78	4T	MFWD, Front hitch/PTO extra		2651	4AC	South Africa
				2850-86	4T	MFWD, Front hitch/PTO extra		2951	4T	South Africa
	2950-85	6		3050-92	6	MFWD, Front hitch/PTO extra				
1985	3150-96	6		3350-100	6	MFWD, Front hitch/PTO extra		3351	6AC	South Africa
				3650-114	6T	MFWD, Front hitch/PTO extra		3651	6AC	South Africa
1987			1986	1350-38	3		1987	1445F	3 42 PS	Italy
				1550-46	3	Italian Goldoni build		1745F	3 48 PS	Italy
	2155-46	3		1750-50	3	MFWD available		1845F	3 56 PS	Italy
				1850-56	3	MFWD available		2345F	3T 67 PS	Italy
	2355-56	4		2250-62	4	MFWD available				
				2450-70	4	MFWD available				
	2555-65	4T		2650-78	4T	MFWD available				
	2755-76	4T		2850-86	4T	MFWD available	1988	2850	4T	Argentina
	2955-86	6		3050-92	6	MFWD available				
1988	3155-95	6				MFWD standard				
1991	3055-92	6		3350-100	6	MFWD available		3350	6	Argentina
	3255-100	6T		3650-114	6T	MFWD standard		3550	6T	Argentina
			1988	1950-62	3T	MFWD available				
1989	4055-105	6T	1989	4055-128	6T					
	4255-120	6T		4255-144	6T					
	4455-140	6T		4455-160	6T					
	4555-155	6T				Not available in Europe				
	4755-175	6TA		4755-190	6TA					
	4955-200	6TA		4955-228	6TA					
	4560-155	6T				Not introduced in Europe				
	4760-175	6TA				Not introduced in Europe				
	4960-200	6TA				Not introduced in Europe				
	5200-40	3				Not introduced in Europe				
	5300-50	3				Not introduced in Europe				
	5400-60	3				Not introduced in Europe				
1992				6100-75	4	2 WD optional, not available in U.S.				
	6200-66	4T		6200-84	4T	2 WD optional				
	6300-75	4T		6300-90	4T	2 WD optional				
	6400-85	4T		6400-100	4T	2 WD optional				
1993	7200-92	6T		6600-110	6T	Not available U.S.				
	7400-100	6T		6800-120	6T	Not available U.S.	1994	2000	3	Czech Republic
1992	7600-110	6T		7600-130	6T	2 WD optional		2100	4	Czech Republic
	7700-125	6T		7700-150	6T	2 WD optional		2200	4	Czech Republic
	7800-145	6T		7800-170	6T	2 WD optional		2300	4	Czech Republic
1994	8100-160	6TA		8100-185	6TA	2 WD optional		2400	4T	Czech Republic
	8200-180	6TA		8200-210	6TA	2 WD optional		2700	4T	Czech Republic
	8300-200	6TA		8300-230	6TA	2 WD optional		2800	4T	Czech Republic
	8400-225	6TA		8400-260	6TA	MFWD standard		2900	4T	Czech Republic

Notes:
NA = Naturally aspirated.
T = Turbocharged.
TA = Turbocharged and aftercooled.
AC = Altitude compensated.

229

A-2 U.S. Tractor Specifications
Waterloo Diesel Tractors

Model	Transmission*	Engine Cylinders†	Bore & Stroke	Displacement (cu. in.)	Rated rpm	Wheel Base (in.)	Rear Tires‡	Hitch Lift (lb)	Sound Level dB(A)§
3020	8 SR	4	4.25x4.75	270	2,500	93	15.5-38		OS
7200	12 SP	6T	4.19x4.33	359	2,100	103	16.9-38	7,400	72.0 cab
4020	8 SR	6	4.25x4.75	404	2,500	100	16.9-38		OS
7400	12 SP	6T	4.19x5.00	414	2,100	103	16.9-38	7,400	72.0 cab
4055	16 QR	6T	4.57x4.75	466	2,200	107	18.4-34D	6,550	76.0 cab
7600	16 PQ	6T	4.19x5.00	414	2,100	110	18.4-38D	7,725	72.0 cab
4255	16 QR	6T	4.57x4.75	466	2,200	107	18.4-38D	6,550	76.5 cab
7700	16 PQ	6T	4.57x4.75	466	2,100	110	18.4-38D	8,925	72.0 cab
4455	16 QR	6T	4.57x4.75	466	2,200	107	18.4-42D	6,550	76.0 cab
7800	16 PQ	6T	4.57x4.75	466	2,100	110	18.4-42D	8,925	72.0 cab
4555	16 QR	6T	4.57x4.75	466	2,200	118	18.4-42D	8,870	76.0 cab
4560	16 QR	6T	4.57x4.75	466	2,200	118	18.4-42D	10,041	76.0 cab
8100	16 PS	6TA	4.57x4.75	466	2,200	122.8	20.8R42	10,400	75.0 cab
4755	16 QR	6TA	4.57x4.75	466	2,200	118	20.8-38D	8,870	76.0 cab
4760	16 QR	6TA	4.57x4.75	466	2,200	118	20.8-42D	10,041	76.0 cab
8200	16 PS	6TA	4.57x4.75	466	2,200	122.8	20.8R42	10,400	75.0 cab
4955	15 PS	6TA	4.57x4.75	466	2,200	118	20.8-42D	9,710	76.5 cab
4960	15 PS	6TA	4.57x4.75	466	2,200	118	20.8-42D	11,773	76.5 cab
8300	16 PS	6TA	4.57x4.75	466	2,200	122.8	20.8R42	11,700	75.0 cab
6030	8 SR	6TA	4.75x5.00	531	2,100	104	20.8-38	5,910	OS
8400	16 PS	6TA	4.57x5.06	496	2,200	116.1	710/70R38	11,700	75.0 cab
8010	9 SM	6	4.25x5.00	425	2,100	120	23.1-26	N/A	OS
8560	24 P	6TA	4.57x4.75	466	2,100	134	18.4-42D	13,940	76.5 cab
8570	12 SR	6TA	4.57x4.75	7.6L	2,100	134	18.4-42D	14,983	74.0 cab
WA14	10 SG	6	5.50x6.00	855	2,100	136	18.4x34	N/A	N/A
WA17	10 SG	6	5.50x6.00	855	2,100	140	28.5x26	N/A	N/A
8760	24 P	6TA	5.12x5.00	619	2,100	134	18.4-42D	13,940	76.0 cab
8770	24 P	6TA	5.12x5.00	10.1L	2,100	134	18.4-42D	14,983	73.5 cab
8850	16 QR	V8TA	5.51x5.00	955	2,100	133	24.5-32D	10,118	78.0 cab
8870	12 SR	6TA	5.12x5.00	10.1L	2,100	134	20.8-42D	12,136	73.5 cab
8960	24 P	6TA	5.50x6.00	855	1,900	134	20.8-42D	13,940	74.0 cab
8970	24 P	6TA	5.50x6.00	14.0L	2,100	134	20.8-42D	N/A	74.0 cab

Notes:
* Transmission lists number of forward speeds and type: SR Syncro-Range, SM Syncro-Mesh, QR Quad-Range, PS power shift, P PowrSync, or SP SyncroPlus.
† Engine cylinders show number and aspiration: T turbocharged or TA turbocharged and aftercooled.
‡ Rear tires show size of test tires followed by "D" if duals were used.
§ OS open station.

230

A-3 Tractor Specifications
Augusta, Yanmar, Mannheim, Goldoni, Saltillo, Rosario, Nigel & Welshpool

Model	Transmission*	Cylinders†	Engine Bore & Stroke (mm)	Displacement (cc)	Rated rpm	Wheel-base (mm)	Rear Tires	Hitch Lift at 24 in. behind (lb)	Sound Level dB(A)‡	RG/Cab/Open Stat.§
Horicon										
655	Infn	3	66x64.2	659	3,200	1,295	7.2-16	825	85.2	RG
755	Infn	3	72x72	878	3,200	1,448	8.3-16	825	89	RG
855	Infn	3	75x75	994	3,200	1,625	9.5-16	825	81	Cab
955	Infn	3	84x86	1,430	3,200	1,625	11.2-16	957	82	Cab
Augusta										
5200	9 CS	3	106.4x110	2,934	2,400	2,050	16.9-28	3,374	83.5	RG
5300	9 CS	3	106.4x110	2,934	2,400	2,050	16.9-28	3,374	84.5	RG
5400	9 CS	3	106.4x110	2,934	2,400	2,050	16.9-30	3,374	81	RG
Yanmar										
900	8 SG	3	80x85	1,281	2,600	1,850	11.2-28	1,765	N/A	RG
670	8 SG	3	72x72	878.5	2,850	1,425	9.5-16	790	85	RG
770	8 SG	3	82x86	1,368	2,600	1,550	11.2-16	815	87	RG
870	9 SG	3	84x86	1,430	2,600	1,714	11.2-24	1,880	86	RG
970	9 CS	4	82x86	1,816	2,600	1,750	11.2-24	2,020	90	RG
1070	9 CS	4	84x86	1,906	2,700	1,750	13.6-28	2,020	90	RG

Mannheim Diesel Tractors

Model	Transmission*	Cylinders†	Engine Bore & Stroke	Displacement (cu. in.)	Rated rpm	Wheel-base (in)	Rear Tires	Shipping Weight (lb)	Hitch Lift (lb)	Sound Level dB(A)‡	RG/Cab/Open Stat.§
100	6 SSG	2	3.67x3.5	72.5	2,500	73.2	10-24	2,750			
300	10 CM	4	3.67x3.5	145	2,000	74.2	11-28	4,035			
500	10 CM	4	3.67x3.5	145	2,400	74.2	11-28	4,540			
700	10 CM	4	3.86x3.5	165	2,400	86.6	11-32	4,774			
10 Series											
200	6 SSG	2	3.86x3.5	82.4	2,500	76.0	10-28	3,252			
310	10 CM	3	3.86x4.33	151.9	2,000	81.5	11-28	4,620			
510	10 CM	3	3.86x4.33	151.9	2,400	81.5	11-32	4,686			
710	10 CM	4	3.86x4.33	202.6	2,400	86.6	11-36	5,049			
20 Series											
820	8 CS	3	3.86x4.33	151.9	2,100	74.4	11-28	4,350			
920	8 CS	3	3.86x4.33	151.9	2,300	74.4	11-28	4,350			
1020	8 CS	3	3.86x4.33	151.9	2,500	80.7	12-28	4,440			
1120	8 CS	3	4.02x4.33	164.4	2,500	80.7	11-36	4,425			
2020	8 CS	4	3.86x4.33	202.6	2,500	85.8	12-36	4,750			
2120	8 CS	4	4.02x4.33	219.0	2,500	85.8	13-38	5,300			
3120	12 CS/HL	6	3.86x4.33	303.0	2,200	96.9	14-34	7,555			
30 Series											
830	8 CS	3	3.86x4.33	151.9	2,400	74.4	12-28	4,509	3,726		RG
930	8 CS	3	3.86x4.33	151.9	2,500	74.4	12-28	4,509	3,726		RG
1030	8 CS	3	4.02x4.33	164.4	2,500	80.7	12-28	4,715	4,025	89	OPU
1130	8 CS	3	4.02x4.33	164.4	2,500	80.7	11-36	4,780	4,025	88	OPU
1630	8 CS	3	4.19x4.33	179.0	2,500	80.7	12-36	4,674	4,100	88	OPU
2030	8 CS	4	4.02x4.33	219.0	2,500	85.8	12-38	5,170	5,565		OPU
2130	8 CS	4	4.19x4.33	239.0	2,500	85.75	15-30	5,725	5,565	87.5	OPU
3030	12 CS/HL	6	4.02x4.33	329.0	2,500	96.9	14-34	7,300	7,455		OPU
3130	12 CS/HL	6	4.02x4.33	329.0	2,500	96.9	15-34	7,300	7,455	85.5	OPU
40 Series											
840	8 CS	3	4.19x4.33	179.0	2,400	74.4	12-28	2,490	4,880		RG
940	8 CS	3	4.19x4.33	179.0	2,400	74.4	13-28	2,490	4,880		RG
1040	8 CS	3	4.19x4.33	179.0	2,500	80.7	11-32	4,616	5,285		OPU
1140	8 CS	3	4.19x4.33	179.0	2,500	80.7	12-36	4,719	5,285		OPU
1640	8 SY	4	4.19x4.33	239.0	2,500	89.7	12-36	7,020	6,770	79	SG2
2040	8 SY	4	4.19x4.33	239.0	2,500	89.7	12-38	7,145	6,770	79	SG2
2040S	8 SY	4	4.19x4.33	239.0	2,500	89.7	12-38	7,365	8,000	79	SG2

A-3 Augusta, Yanmar, Mannheim, Goldoni, Saltillo, Rosario, Nigel & Welshpool (continued)

Model	Transmission*	Cylinders†	Bore & Stroke	Displacement (cu. in.)	Rated rpm	Wheel-base (in.)	Rear Tires	Shipping Weight (lb)	Hitch Lift (lb)	Sound Level dB(A)‡	RG/ Cab/ Open Stat.§
2140	8 SY	4T	4.19x4.33	239.0	2,500	89.7	12-38	7,620	8,000	79	SG2
3040	16 PS	6	4.19x4.33	359.0	2,500	100.4	14-38	9,175	9,040	79	SG2
3140	16 PS	6	4.19x4.33	359.0	2,500	100.4	15-34	9,175	9,040	79.5	SG2
3640	16 PS	6	4.19x4.33	359.0	2,400	102.0	15-38	10,564	7,930	80.5	SG2
4040S	16 QR	6T	4.19x4.33	359.0	2,200	103.9	15-38	11,067	10,185		SG2
4240S	16 QR	6T	4.56x4.75	466.0	2,200	106.6	15-38	11,596	11,960		SG2
4350	16 QR	6T	4.56x4.75	466.0	2,200	105.3	15-38	MFWD-14,090	12,260	80	SG2
			(mm)	(cc)		(mm)					
50 Series											
1350	8 SY	3	106.5x110	2,940	2,300	2,050	12.4-28	5,358	2,070		RG
1550	8 SY	3	106.5x110	2,940	2,300	2,050	12.4-28	5,821	2,070		MC1
1750	8 SY	3	106.5x110	2,940	2,300	2,050	12.4-32	5,998	2,070		MC1
1850	8 SY	3	106.5x110	2,940	2,400	2,150	13.6-36	5,612	2,584		MC1
1950	8 SY	3T	106.5x110	2,940	2,300	2,150	16.9-28	6,152	3,438	83	MC1
50-6000 Series											
2250	8 SY	4	106.5x110	3,920	2,300	2,266	13.6-24	7,486	3,438		SG2
2450	8 SY	4	106.5x110	3,920	2,300	2,266	16.9-30	7,486	3,438		SG2
6100	12 SY	4	106.5x127	4,530	2,300	2,400	16.9R34	7,840 MFWD-8,600	4,593	75	TCr
2650	8 SY	4T	106.5x110	3,920	2,300	2,266	13.6-38	7,695	3,720		SG2
6200	12 SY	4T	106.5x110	3,920	2,300	2,400	16.9R38	7,927 MFWD-8,710	5,025	72.5	TCr
2850	8 SY	4T	106.5x110	3,920	2,500	2,266	13.6-38	8,202	4,388	77.5	SG2
6300	12 SY	4T	106.5x110	3,920	2,300	2,400	16.9R38	8,004 MFWD-8,810	5,850	73	TCr
3050	8 TSS	6	106.5x110	5,883	2,300	2,551	16.9-38	11,543	5,235	79.5	SG2
6400	12 SP	4T	106.5x127	4,530	2,300	2,400	16.9R38	8,246 MFWD-9,040	6,950	73.5	TCr
3350	8 TSS	6	106.5x110	5,883	2,300	2,551	18.4-38	MFWD-12,244	5,235	77.5	SG2
6600	20 PQ	6T	106.5x110	5,883	2,300	2,847	18.4R38	MFWD-10,253	7,363	75	TCr
3650	16 TSS	6T	106.5x110	5,883	2,400	2,551	18.4-38	MFWD-13,909	6,308	80.5	SG2
6800	16 PQ	6T	106.5x127	6,786	2,100	2,847	20.8R38	MFWD-11,003	8,153	75	TCr
Goldoni								Weight (lb) 2WD/MFWD			
445	8 SY	3				1,810		/			OS
604	8 SY	3	100x105	2,472	2,600	1,810	12.4-24	/4,245			OS
614	8 SY	3	105x105	2,780	2,600	1,810	14.9-24	/			OS
1445F	8 SY	3	106.5x110	2,940	2,300	1,835	11.2-24	4,057/4,278			RG
1745F	8 SY	3	106.5x110	2,940	2,300	1,835	12.4-24	4,057/4,278			RG
1845F	8 SY	3	106.5x110	2,940	2,400	1,835	14.5-20	4,057/4,278			RG
2345F	8 SY	3T	106.5x110	2,940	2,300	1,835	14.5-20	4,057/4,278			RG
EUR42	6	3		1,551	3,000	1,220	8.25-16	– /2,866			RG
EUR50	6	3		1,871	3,000	1,220	8.25-16	– /2,977			RG
Saltillo											
2535	8 CS	4	102x110	3,588	2,500		15.5-38	5,732			OS
2735	8 CS	4	106.5x110	3,916	2,500		18.4-30	6,834			OS
4235	8 SR	6	108x120	6,620	2,200		18.4-34	11,067			OS
4435T	8 SR	6T	115.8x120.7	6,620	2,200		20.8-34	12,302			OS
2555	8 CS	4	106.5x110	3,916	2,500		14.9-38	5,952			OS
2755	8 CS	4	106.5x110	3,916	2,500		15.5-38	6,228			OS
2755T	8 CS	4T	106.5x110	3,916	2,500		18.4-30	7,639			OS
2755TS	8 TSS	4T	106.5x110	3,916	2,500		18.4-34	8,454			OS
4255	8 SR	6T	115.8x120.7	7,636	2,200		18.4-34	12,028			OS
4455	8 SR	6T	115.8x120.7	7,636	2,200		20.8-34	12,412			OS
Rosario											
730S	6 SG	2	155.6x177.8	6,161	1,125	2,092	12-38	3,532			OS
445S	5 SG	2	98.4x114.3	1,737	1,850	2,184	13-28	2,096			OS
1420	5 SR	3	102x110	2,695	2,200	2,210	13.6-28	2,334			OS
2420	8 SR	4	102x110	3,580	2,500	2,290	18.4-30	4,342			OS
3420	8 SR	6	97.6x110	4,960	2,500	2,550	18.4-34	5,441			OS
4420	8 SR	6	102x110	5,390	2,500	2,550	23.1-30	5,441			OS

A-3 Augusta, Yanmar, Mannheim, Goldoni, Saltillo, Rosario, Nigel & Welshpool (continued)

Model	Transmission*	Cylinders†	Engine Bore & Stroke	Displacement (cc)	Rated rpm	Wheel-base (mm)	Rear Tires	Shipping Weight (lb)	Hitch Lift (lb)	RG/ Cab/ Open Stat.§
Rosario										
2330	8 CS	3	102x110	2,696	2,500	2,050	13.6-28		3,500	OS
2530	8 CS	4	102x110	3,598	2,500	2,170	18.4-30	3,500		OS
2730	8 CS	4	106.5x110	3,920	2,500	2,180	18.4-30	4,397		OS
3330	8 SY	4	106.5x110	3,920	2,500	2,370	18.4-34	4,733		OS
3530	8 SY	6	102x110	5,390	2,500	2,630	18.4-34	5,600		OS
4530	8 SR	6	106.5x110	5,883	2,500	2,630	23.1-30		5,600	OS
2140	8 SY	4T	106.5x110	3,920	2,500	2,280	18.4-30	4,390		OS
3140	8 SY	6	106.5x110	5,883	2,500	2,550	18.4-34		6,500	OS
3540	8 SY	6T	106.5x110	5,883	2,400	2,580	18.4-38		6,500	OS
4040	8 SR	6	107.9x120.7	6,620	2,200	2,640	23.1-30	4,368		RG
4050	16 QR	6	115.8x120.7	7,636	2,200	2,675	23.1-30	5,029		RG
2850	8 SY	4T	106.5x110	3,920	2,300	2,280	18.4-34	4,430		OS
3350	8 SY	6	106.5x110	5,883	2,300	2,555	18.4-34		6,510	OS
3550	8 SY	6T	106.5x110	5,883	2,400	2,590	18.4-38		6,510	OS

Model	Transmission*	Cylinders†	Engine Bore & Stroke	Displacement (cc)	Rated rpm	Wheel-base (mm)	Rear Tires	Weight (lb) 2WD/MFWD	Hitch Lift (lb)	RG/ Cab/ Open Stat.§
Nigel										
1641	8 TSS	4NA	98.4x127	3,860	2,300	2,285	16.9-30	2,478/2,733	4,766	OS
2141	8 TSS	4AC	98.4x127	3,860	2,300	2,285	18.4-34	2,828/2,968	5,620	OS
2541	8 TSS	4T	98.4x127	3,860	2,300	2,285	18.4-34	2,828/2,968	5,620	OS
2941	8 TSS	4T	98.4x127	3,860	2,300	2,285	18.4-38	3,740/3,910	7,643	OS
3141	8 TSS	6AC	98.4x127	5,800	2,300	2,580	18.4-38	4,160/4,300	7,643	OS
2251	8 TSS	4NA	98.4x127	3,860	2,300	2,335	16.9-30	2,560/2,830	4,991	OS
2351	8 TSS	4AC	98.4x127	3,860	2,300	2,335	16.9-30	2,560/2,830	4,991	OS
2651	16 PSY	4AC	98.4x127	3,860	2,300	2,335	18.4-34	2,830/2,970	5,912	OS
2951	16 PSY	4T	98.4x127	3,860	2,300	2,335	18.4-34	3,750/3,920	7,756	OS
3351	16 PSY	6AC	98.4x127	5,800	2,300	2,580	18.4-38	4,280/4,460	7,756	OS
3651	16 PSY	6AC	98.4x127	5,800	2,300	2,580	20.8-38	– / 4,550	7,756	OS

Model	Transmission*	Cylinders†	Engine Bore & Stroke (in.)	Displacement (cu. in.)	Rated rpm	Wheel-base (mm)	Rear Tires	Weight as tested/ shipping (lb)	Sound Level dB(A)‡	RG/ Cab/ Open Stat.§
Welshpool										
40K	9	2	6.12x6.25	199	1,200	2,108	13.5-32	8,500		OS
40KA	9	2	6.12x6.25	199	1,200	2,108	18.4-30	9,044		OS
45KA	9	2	6.12x6.25	199	1,200	2,108	18.4-30	9,044		OS
55KA	9	2	6.625x6.25	215	1,200	2,108	18.4-30	9,000		OS
55D/DA	9	2	6.625x6.25	215	1,200	2,108	18.4-30			OS
60DA	9	3	4.25x5.0	213	1,500		18.4-30			OS
Super 70	9	3	4.25x5.0	213	1,500		18.4-30			OS
Super 90	9	3	4.25x5.0	213	1,500		23.1-26			OS
Countryman 6	9	6	3.87x5.0	354	2,200		23.1-26			OS
Countryman 354	9	6	3.87x5.0	354	2,200		23.1-26			OS
Countryman C6100	9	6	3.87x5.0	354	2,200		23.1-26	12,270		OS
Champion 6G	9	4	4.25x4.75	270	2,000		18.4-30			OS
Champion 9G	9	4	4.25x4.75	270	2,000		18.4-30			OS
Champion 236	9	4	4.25x4.75	270	2,000		18.4-30			OS
Champion 239	9	4	4.19x4.33	239	2,000		18.4-30			OS
Champion 306	9	6	3.6x5.0	306	2,000	2,261	18.4-30	9,850		OS
Champion C670	9	6	3.6x5.0	306	2,000	2,261	18.4-30	9,850		OS
Crusader	9	4	4.25x4.75	270	2,000		18.4-30			OS
Canelander	9	4	4.25x4.75	270	1,800	2,254	14.9-38	9,460		OS
Canelander AP	9	6	3.6x5.0	306	2,000					OS
3380/B	12	4	4.19x4.33	239	2,500		23.1-26	9,433/ 9,658	85	Sedan
4080/B	12	6	4.02x4.33	329	2,200		23.1-30	10,050/10,050	85	Sedan
4280/B	12	6	4.19x4.33	359	2,500		23.1-34	12,475/12,238	85	Sedan
4480/B	12	6T	4.19x4.33	359	2,500		24.5-32	13,238/13,739	85	Sedan
4090/MFWD	12	6	4.19x4.33	359	2,200	2,570	18.4-38	11,671/12,302	78	SG
4290/MFWD	12	6T	4.19x4.33	359	2,200	2,903	24.5-32	13,228/13,785	78	SG
4490/MFWD	12	6T	4.57x4.75	466	2,200	2,903	24.5-32	13,779/14,319	78	SG
4690/MFWD	12	6T	4.57x4.75	466	2,200	2,903	24.5-32	13,779/14,639	78	SG

A-3 Augusta, Yanmar, Mannheim, Goldoni, Saltillo, Rosario, Nigel & Welshpool (continued)

Model	Engine hp	Transmission*	Cylinders†	Engine Bore & Stroke (mm)	Displacement (cu. in.)	Rated rpm	2WD (lb)	Rear Tires	Shipping Weight (lb)	Sound Level dB(A)‡	RG/Cab
Brno											
2000	49	10 SY	3	102x110	2,691	2,200	2,123	14.9-28	2,380	84	Cab
2100	62	10 SY	4	100x110	3,460	2,200	2,257	14.9-28	2,560	84	Cab
2200	68	10 SY	4	102x110	3,588	2,200	2,257	16.9-28	2,595	84	Cab
2300	74	10 SY	4	102x120	3,900	2,200	2,257	16.9-30	2,615	84	Cab
2400	81	10 SY	4T	102x120	3,900	2,200	2,257	16.9-34	2,615	84	Cab
2700	89	8 SY	4T	105x120	4,200	2,200	2,376	16.9-38	3,068	82/3	SG
2800	100	8 SY	4T	105x120	4,200	2,200	2,376	16.9-38	3,201	82/3	SG
2900	106	8 SY	4T	105x120	4,200	2,200	2,376	18.4-38	3,201	82/3	SG

Notes:
* Transmission lists number of forward speeds and type: SG sliding gear, SSG selective sliding gear, CS collar shift, TSS top shaft synchronized, SR Syncro-Range, QR Quad-Range, PS Power Shift, PQ PowerQuad, or SP SyncroPlus.
† Engine cylinders show number and T if turbocharged.
‡ Sound level is at the operator's ear at 75% load.
§ OS open station, RG Roll-Gard ROPS, Cabs: SG/SG2 Sound-Gard/(2), MC1 Minimum-Clearance, CC2 Console-Comfort, TCr TechCenter.

A-4 U.S. Tractor Specifications
U.S.-Mannheim Built Diesel Tractors

Model	Transmission*	Cylinders†	Engine Bore & Stroke	Displacement (cu. in.)	Rated rpm	Wheelbase (in.)	Rear Tires	Hitch Lift (lb)	Sound Level dB(A)‡	RG/Cab
Mannheim										
2150	8 CS	3	4.19x4.33	179	2,500	75	16.9-28	2,023	93.0	RG
2155	8 CS	3	4.19x4.33	179	2,500	81	16.9-28	2,584	94.0	RG
2350	8 CS	4	4.19x4.33	239	2,500	89	16.9-30	2,736	93.5	RG
2355	8 CS	4	4.19x4.33	239	2,500	89	16.9-30	3,438	93.5	RG
2550	8 CS	4	4.19x4.33	239	2,500	89	18.4-30	2,736	95.0	RG
2555	8 CS	4	4.19x4.33	239	2,500	89	18.4-30	3,439	97.0	RG
6200	12 SP	4T	4.19x4.33	239	2,300	94.5	15.5-38	5,025	75.0	Cab
2750	8 CS	4T	4.19x4.33	239	2,500	89	18.4-30	3,372	93.5	RG
2755	8 CS	4T	4.19x4.33	239	2,500	89	18.4-30	3,720	76.5	Cab
6300	12 SP	4T	4.19x4.33	239	2,300	94.5	15.5-38	5,850	75.0	Cab
2950	16 TSS	6	4.19x4.33	359	2,500	100	18.4-38	4,868	76.0	Cab
2955	8 TSS	6	4.19x4.33	359	2,300	100	18.4-38	5,235	77.0	Cab
3055	16 TSS	6	4.19x4.33	359	2,300	100	18.4-38	5,235	79.5	Cab
6400	12 SP	4T	4.19x5.00	276	2,300	94.5	16.9-38	6,950	75.0	Cab
3150	16 TSS	6T	4.19x4.33	359	2,400	102	18.4-38	6,300	77.5	Cab
3155	16 TSS	6T	4.19x4.33	359	2,400	102	18.4-38	6,308	77.5	Cab
3255	16 TSS	6T	4.19x4.33	359	2,400	102	18.4-38	6,308	80.5	Cab

Notes:
* The transmission lists number of forward speeds and type: SG sliding gear, CS collar shift, TSS top shaft synchronized, SR Syncro-Range, or SP SyncroPlus.
† Engine cylinders show number and T if turbocharged.
‡ Sound level is at the operator's ear at 75% load.

A-5 Nebraska Tractor Tests
Waterloo Diesel Tractors

Model	Year	Test No	Max PTO (hp)	Maximum Drawbar (hp at mph)		Maximum Pull (lb)	Weight with Ballast (lb)	Max. PTO hp at Std PTO rpm (hp-h/gal)	75% of Pull at Max Power (hp-h/gal)
3020	1963	848	65.3	57.1	5.0	7,536	9,585	13.85	10.61
7200	1994								
4020	1963	849	91.2	63.3	4.9	10,184	13,055	14.89	11.77
7400	1994								
4055	1989	064	108.7	99.1	4.3	13,378	13,660	16.1	13.4
7600	1991	131	111.6	93.52	4.14	14,507	14,989	17.53	13.02
4255	1989	065	123.7	111.9	6.0	14,635	14,805	16.5	13.8
7700	1991	134	126.1	115.6	4.51	14,836	16,810	15.88	13.21
4455	1989	066	142.7	128.8	5.6	17,161	17,210	17.0	14.1
7800	1991	136	146.7	136.0	4.59	14,866	19,050	17.08	13.55
4555	1989	067	156.8	141.8	5.7	17,774	18,745	17.4	14.5
4560	1991	—	156.8	141.8	5.7	17,774	18,745	17.4	14.5
4755	1989	068	177.1	156.0	7.1	19,898	20,320	18.2	15.4
4760	1991	—	177.1	156.0	7.1	19,898	20,320	18.2	15.4
4955	1989	060	202.7	173.5	3.9	23,742	24,665	18.4	14.6
4960	1991	—	202.7	173.5	3.9	23,742	24,665	18.4	14.6
6030	1972	1100	176.0	155.4	6.6	21,530	18,180	15.8	12.7
8010	No NB Test		215	150 est.			24,860		
8560	1989	061	202.6	180.7	6.1	32,166	32,075	17.2	14.1
8570	1993	138	230.84	210.36	4.99	31,924	32,265	17.46	15.23
WA14	No NB Test		N/A	N/A					
WA17	No NB Test		N/A	N/A					
8760	1989	1062	256.9	240.2	4.6	32,880	32,695	16.3	14.0
8770	1993	139	259.31	286.31	4.95	33,464	33,124	16.7	14.67
8850	1982	1434	304.0	274.2	5.2	35,330	37,700	15.7	13.3
8870	1993	140	335.69	307.58	4.39	35,026	35,295	18.0	14.95
8960	1989	063	333.4	308.2	5.9	34,316	35,570	17.1	14.3
8970	1993	141	393.39	348.12	5.65	34,302	33,820	18.27	14.66

Sources: *Nebraska Tractor Test Data*, *Implement & Tractor Red Book*, and *Official Guide, Tractors and Farm Equipment*.

A-6 Nebraska/OECD Tractor Tests
U.S.-Mannheim-Built Diesel Tractors

Model	Year	Test No.	Maximum PTO (hp)	Maximum Drawbar (hp at mph)		Maximum Pull (lb)	Weight with Ballast (lb)	Fuel Use at: Max. PTO hp at Standard PTO rpm (hp-h/gal)	75% of Pull at Max. Power (hp-h/gal)
Mannheim									
2150	1983	1469	46.5	38.7	7.0	4,875	5,930	14.8	11.2
2155	1987	024	45.6	37.4	7.7	3,975	5,300	15.3	11.7
2350	1983	1470	56.2	47.3	6.8	5,688	7,190	15.7	11.9
2355	1987	025	55.9	46.7	8.2	6,195	6,965	16.3	12.6
6100	1992	296	51.3 kW	44.0 kW	7.73 km/h	52.98 kN	6,725 kg	12.11kg/h	9.85 kg/h
2550	1983	1471	65.9	56.2	6.2	6,979	8,485	15.4	12.1
2555	1987	027	66.0	56.5	5.7	6,910	7,300	16.4	13.2
6200	1992	292	58.1 kW	50.1 kW	7.41 km/h	60.55 kN	6,725 kg	13.14 kg/h	10.15 kg/h
2750	1983	1472	75.4	64.0	4.8	7,581	9,625	16.1	12.4
2755	1986	1605	76.6	66.0	5.2	7,498	9,715	17.8	14.2
6300	1992	171	63.3 kW	52.8 kW	7.56 km/h	73.33 kN	7,425 kg	14.05 kg/h	10.71 kg/h
2950	1983	1473	85.4	73.3	6.7	8,768	11,045	16.3	12.4
2955	1986	1606	86.2	74.2	5.4	9,971	11,150	17.4	13.8
3055	1991	100	94.4	81.8	7.4	12,055	14,770	17.56	13.8
6400	1994	222	68.0 kW	58.1 kW	5.59 km/h	74.07 kN	7,425 kg	15.17 kg/h	11.76 kg/h
3150	1986	1589	96.1	83.0	5.1	10,507	12,300	16.4	13.3
3155	1986	1589	96.1	83.0	5.1	10,507	12,300	16.4	13.3
3255	1991	101	102.6	89.2	3.95	16,905	18,300	16.85	13.55
6600	1994								
6800	1994								

Sources: *Nebraska Tractor Test Data*, OECD Standard Test Data, *Implement & Tractor Red Book*, and *Official Guide, Tractors and Farm Equipment.*

A-7 Tractor Tests
Augusta and Mannheim Diesel Tractors

Model	Year	Test No.	Maximum PTO (hp)	Maximum Drawbar (hp at mph)		Maximum Pull (lb)	Weight with Ballast (lb)	Max. PTO hp at Std PTO rpm (hp-h/gal)	75% of Pull at Max. Power (hp-h/gal)
Augusta									
5200	1992	115	41.12	36.03	4.02	5,851	6,130	16.28	13.10
5300	1992	116	50.67	43.44	3.91	6,285	7,154	16.39	13.64
5400	1992	117	60.67	54.33	7.57	6,895	8,006	17.19	13.58
Mannheim									
1350	No Test								
1750	1987	7270C	45.59				6,691		
[2155	1988	048]	16.10	37.4	4.67	5,625	5,975	15.84	11.88
2250	1983	1469	46.5	38.7	7.0	4,875	5,930	14.8	11.20
[2355	1987	026]	56.60	48.5	5.00	7,680	7,695	17.11	13.55
2450	1986	6205C	63.83				8,179		
[2555	1987	027]	66.00	56.5	5.66	6,910	7,300	16.40	13.25
6100	1992-93	1460E	68.79	59.0	4.8	11,910	14,826	17.61	14.26
(2WD)			(51.3 kW	44.0 kW	7.73 k/h	52.98 kN	6,725 kg	3.72 kW-h/L	2.81 kW-h/L)
2650	1987	028	65.6	56.5	5.1	8,055	8,080	17.26	13.65
[2555	1987	027]	65.6	56.5	5.1	8,055	8,080	17.26	13.65
6200	1993	1461E	77.91	67.05	4.6	13,612	14,826	16.04	13.55
(4WD)			(58.1 kW	50.1 kW	7.41 k/h	60.55 kN	6,725 kg	3.72 kW-h/L	3.05 kW-h/L)
2850	1986	1021E	82.47	70.13	4.92	13,194	13,040	17.87	15.58
6300	1992	1447E	84.88	70.80	4.7	16,485	16,369	18.43	15.23
(4WD)			(63.3 kW	52.8 kW	7.56 k/h	73.33 kN	7,425 kg	3.63 kW-h/L	3.00 kW-h/L)
3050	1986	1606	86.22	74.2	5.42	9,971	11,150	17.18	13.79
6400	1992	1427E	91.19	77.91	3.47	16,651	16,369	18.53	13.70
(4WD)			(68.0 kW	58.8 kW	7.33 k/h	74.07 kN	7,425 kg	3.65 kW-h/L	3.07 kW-h/L)
3350	1986	100	96.1	83.0	5.6	10,507	12,300	16.4	13.30
6600	1994								
3650	1991	101	110.9	99.81	7.41	11,111	14,810	17.17	14.08
6800	1994								

Sources: OECD Tractor Test Data (E), Cemagref Tractor Test Data (C), *Nebraska Tractor Test Data, Implement & Tractor Red Book*, and *Official Guide, Tractors and Farm Equipment.*

A-8 Production Years and Serial Numbers

LANZ, Mannheim	Years Built	Series		PS	Serial Numbers		Series	Years Built	Model	PS	Serial Numbers
Landbaumotor	1911-17	LB/LC		80	1 -	120	20 series	1967-75	820	32	10,000 - 100,700
Landbaumotor	1919-26	LD I/II/III		80	1,001 -	1,500		1967-75	920	37	1,000 - 181,045
Fieldinstmotor	1919-23	FMA-FMD		20-38	130 -	426		1967-75	1020	44	1,000 - 180,698
Felddank	1925-27	FHD		38	50,001 -	52,000		1967-75	1120	49	10,000 - 181,046
Bulldog	1921-27	HL		12	1,501 -	6,500		1967-75	2020	60	10,000 - 90,200
Bulldog	1921-27	HL		12	17,001 -	17,932		1968-75	2120	68	23,019 - 90,200
Bulldog	1921-27	HL		12	18,230 -	18,328		1969-75	3120	81	35,903 - 90,200
Bulldog	1923-25	HM		8	20,001 -	20,250					
Field-Bulldog 4WD	1923-26	HP		12	6,501 -	7,223	30 series	1975-79	830	35	155,503 - 335,747
							(new style)	1975-79	930	41	182,552 - 335,770
Gros-Bulldog	1926-31	HR2		22/28	45,001 -	50,000	(new style)	1975-79	1030	46	181,807 - 338,577
(Hopper-cooled)		HR2		22/28	52,001 -	54,230	(new style)	1975-79	1130	51	181,928 - 336,721
Kuhler-Bulldog	1928-29	HR4		30	75,001 -	75,180	(original style)	1973-79	1630	56	189,681 - 338,589
(Radiator-cooled)	1929-35	HR5/6	D6500	15/30	75,181 -	86,681	(original style)	1972-79	18/2030	68	156,832 - 307,411
Row-crop/Standard	1932-34	HN1	D7500	12/20	100,001 -	100,678	(original style)	1972-79	2130	79	155,483 - 339,206
Standard	1934-35	HN2	D7511	20	100,679 -	101,272	(original style)	1978-79	3030	86	282,403 - 339,200
	1935-52	HN3/4	D7500	20	110,001 -	125,000	(new style)	1975-79	3130	100	155,474 - 308,445
	1939-52	HN3/4	D7506	20	210,001 -	215,395					
	1942	HN3/4	D7500	20	500,001 -	511,232	40 series	1979-86	840	38	320,001 - 587,092
	1936-52	HN5	D3500	20	175,001 -	188,890		1979-86	940	44	320,006 - 586,994
	1950-52	HN5	D3500	20	527,001 -	531,367		1979-86	1040	50	320,012 - 587,736
	1934-40	HR7/8	D85/9500	30/35	125,001 -	150,000		1979-86	1140	56	320,034 - 587,795
	1940-55	HR7/8	D85/9500	35/45	650,001 -	656,394		1979-86	1640	62	320,072 - 587,930
	1934-55	HR7/8	D1500	55	680,001 -	680,313		1979-86	2040	70	320,096 - 587,423
	1940-47	HRK	D1561	55	700,001 -	702,437		1980-86	2040S	75	388,759 - 587,371
	1936-54	HR9	D2500	55	150,001 -	152,803		1979-86	2140	82	320,122 - 588,421
								1979-86	3040	90	320,156 - 586,848
John Deere-Lanz	1956-58	TWN	D1106 bulli	11	200,010 -	201,049		1979-86	3140	97	320,174 - 587,616
	1958-60	TWN	D1206	12	201,050 -			1984-86	3640	112	524,062 - 588,080
	1955-58	TWN	D1306	13	300,001 -			1981-84	4040S	115	345,012 - 348,075
	1955	MWM	D1266	12	310,001 -	310,452		1981-84	4240S	132	345,029 - 349,018
	1955	MWM	D1666	16	320,001 -	320,601					
	1955-60		D1616	16	160,001 -		50 series	1986-90	1350	38	600,372 - 699,830
	1952-55		D1706	17	270,001 -			1987-94	1550	44	602,057 - 775,373
Alldog	1957-59	MWM	A1806	16	10,003 -			1987-94	1750	50	601,199 - 775,348
	1955		D1906	19	278,001 -	278,600		1986-94	1850	56	600,544 - 775,481
	1955-60		D2016	20	279,001 -			1988-94	1950	65	623,964 - 775,378
	1952-55		D2206	22	540,001 -	546,898		1986-94	2250	62	600,188 - 775,468
	1955		D2216	22	549,001 -	550,000		1986-94	2450	70	600,197 - 775,352
	1956-59		D2402	24	554,002 -			1986-94	2650	78	600,206 - 775,301
	1955-60		D2416	24	550,001 -			1986-94	2850	88	600,057 - 775,448
	1956-59		D2802	28				1986-93	3050	92	600,223 - 747,866
								1986-93	3350	103	600,054 - 775,346
	1953-55	HN	D2803	28				1986-93	3650	116	609,192 - 775,621
	1953-55		D2806	28	220,004 -	224,364		1985-93	4350	140	561,117 - 589,378
	1955-60		D2816	28	330,001 -						
	1953-56		D3206	32	230,001 -		6000 series	1992-	6100	75	100,067 -
	1954-56		D3606	36	660,005 -	663,340		1992-	6200	84	100,070 -
	1956-60		D4016	40	345,006 -			1992-	6300	90	100,081 -
	1954-55		D4806/16	48	711,001 -			1992-	6400	100	100,113 -
	1954-55		D5806/16	58	711,001 -			1994-	6600	110	118,151 -
	1955-59		D5006	50	711,030 -			1993-	6800	120	115,409 -
	1955-56		D5007	50	711,326 -						
	1955-62		D5016	50	725,001 -		MANNHEIM Built:				
	1955-59		D6006	60	711,030 -		55 series U.S.	1987-93	US 2155		601,741 - 770,727
	1955-56		D6007	60	711,418 -			1987-94	US 2355		600,187 - 775,347
	1955-62		D6016	60	725,001 -			1987-94	US 2555		600,175 - 775,353
	1956-62		D6017	60	711,534 -			1986-94	US 2755		600,089 - 775,307
								1988-94	US 2855N		629,463 - 775,423
John Deere-LANZ	1962-65	100		18	15,001 -			1986-92	US 2955		600,180 - 767,516
(multi-cylinder)	1960-65	300		28	50,000 -			1991-93	US 3055		736,829 - 773,476
	1960-65	500		36	100,000 -			1987-91	US 3155		618,645 - 738,221
	1962-65	700		48	150,000 -			1991-93	US 3255		736,426 - 773,706
John Deere	1966-67	310		32	60,001 -	68,264					
	1966-67	510		40	110,001 -	119,235					
	1966-67	710		50	155,001 -	164,605					
	1966-67	200		25	136,200 -						

A-8 Production Years and Serial Numbers (continued)

Date from-to	Model	First		Last
ROSARIO SERIAL NOS:				
12/58 - 08/19/70	730	300,000 -		320,022
01/26/64 - 05/08/70	445	445,000 -		451,020
08/21/70 - 06/10/75	1420	1,000 -		2,906
10/14/70 - 08/13/75	2420	1,000 -		7,412
10/04/70 - 08/18/75	3420	1,000 -		7,332
09/21/70 - 08/18/75	4420	1,000 -		5,666
10/27/75 - 12/08/79	2330	1,000 -		2,309
10/28/75 - 12/10/79	2530	1,000 -		2,378
10/29/75 - 11/28/79	2730	1,000 -		2,931
02/27/79 - 09/15/80	3330	1,000 -		1,678
07/31/75 - 10/09/80	3530	1,000 -		7,074
08/06/75 - 04/02/80	4530	1,000 -		4,846
06/02/83 - 07/18/88	2140	1,001 -		1,732
05/13/83 - 07/14/88	3140	1,218 -		2,843
05/14/86 - 10/14/88	3540	1,001 -		1,240
08/10/88 -	2850	1,003 -		
08/11/88 -	3350	1,003 -		
08/09/88 -	3550	1,003 -		
NIGEL SERIAL NOS:				
1982 - 02/03/87	1641X	-		664
1982 - 03/13/87	1641M	-		217
1982 - 05/28/86	1641F	-		056
1982 - 04/29/87	2141	-		282
1982 - 05/13/87	2141X	-		699
1982 - 01/13/87	2541X	-		081
1982 - 01/29/87	2541M	-		074
1982 - 06/04/87	2941	-		102
1982 - 02/09/87	2941M	-		101
1982 - 08/01/86	3141X	-		289
1982 - 03/24/87	3141M	-		206
04/1987 -	2251			
04/1987 -	2351			
04/1987 -	2651			
04/1987 -	2951			
04/1987 -	3151			

Date from -to	Model	First		Last	Last Off
AUSTRALIAN CHAMBERLAIN SERIAL NOS:					
1949-1955	40K/KA/45K/KA	1 -		1,995	01/55
1954-1956	55K/KA	101 -		365	02/56
1954-1957	55DA	101 -		441	07/57
1952-1954	60DA	1 -		190	01/54
1954-1962	Super 70	191 -		1,200	02/62
1962-1967	Super 90	1,201 -		2,003	05/67
1955-1958	Champion 6G	101 -		1,703	08/58
1958-1966	Champion 9G	1,704 -		8,165	03/66
	(4-L4 engine to s/n 1963)				
	(4-270D engine @ s/n 1964)				
1966-1970	Champion 306	1,001 -		5,060	10/75
1970-1975	Champion 306L/C670	5,061 -		9,962	01/76
1970-1972	Champion 236B (basic)	1,001 -		1,025	08/72
1970-1973	Champion 236D (drawbar)	1,001 -		1,156	06/73
1970-1975	Champion 236L (linkage)	1,001 -		1,534	10/75
1975	Champion 239 (JD eng.)	1,535 -		1,584	
1958-1960	Countryman Mark I & II	1,001 -		1,406	
1960-1962	Countryman Mark III	1,407 -		2,003	11/62
1963-1966	Countryman 6	2,004 -		3,918	12/66
1966-1970	Countryman 354	1,001 -		2,892	
1970-1976	Countryman C6100	2,893 -		5,590	03/76
1959-1967	Canelander	101 -		625	05/67
1968-1972	Canelander AP	1,001 -		1,321	05/72
1959-1963	Crusader	101 -		316	10/63
1972-1974	C456	1,001 -		1,030	01/74
1975-1983	3380	1,001 -		2,316	
1975-1983	4080	1,001 -		2,822	
1975-1983	4280	1,001 -		2,822	
1975-1983	4480	1,001 -		2,844	
1983-1985	3380B	11,001 -		11,205	
1983-1985	4080B D/bar	21,001 -		21,255	
1983-1985	4080B Linkage	31,001 -		31,332	
1983	4080B ROPS	41,001 -		41,029	
1983-1985	4280B D/bar	51,001 -		51,211	
1983-1985	4280B Linkage	61,001 -		61,153	
1983-1985	4480B	71,001 -		71,427	
1985-1986	4090	510 built			
1985-1986	4290	270 built			
1985-1986	4490	250 built			
1985-1986	4690	180 built			

A-9 Chamberlain Tractors

Year	Model	Engine	Model	Engine	Model	Engine	Model	Engine	Model	Engine
1948	40K	2-cyl								
1949	40K	2-cyl								
1950	40K	2-cyl								
1950	40KA	2-cyl								
1951	40KA	2-cyl								
1952	40KA	2-cyl			60DA	GM3.71				
1953	40KA	2-cyl			60DA	GM3.71				
1954	40KA	2-cyl	55D/DA	2-cyl	60DA	GM3.71				
1954	45KA	2-cyl			Super 70	GM3.71				
1955	45KA	2-cyl	55D/DA	2-cyl	(or 70DA)					
1955	55KA	2-cyl			Super 70	GM3.71	Champion 6G	Perkins		
1956	55KA	2-cyl	55D/DA	2-cyl	Super 70	GM3.71	Champion 6G	L4		
1957			55D/DA	2-cyl	Super 70	GM3.71	Champion 6G	L4		
1958	Countryman Mark 1	Meadows			Super 70	GM3.71	Champion 6G	L4		
1959	Countryman Mark 1	4-330	Crusader	Perkins	Super 70	GM3.71	Champion 9G	4-270	Canelander	Perkins
1960	Countryman Mark 2	4-330	Crusader	4-270	Super 70	GM3.71	Champion 9G	4-270	Canelander	4-270
1961	Countryman Mark 3	4-330	Crusader	4-270	Super 70	GM3.71	Champion 9G	4-270	Canelander	4-270
1962	Countryman Mark 3	4-330	Crusader	4-270	Super 70	GM3.71	Champion 9G	4-270	Canelander	4-270
1963	Countryman 6	Perkins			Super 90	GM3.71	Champion 9G	4-270	Canelander	4-270
1964	Countryman 6	6-354			Super 90	GM3.71	Champion 9G	4-270	Canelander	4-270
1965	Countryman 6	6-354			Super 90	GM3.71	Champion 9G	4-270	Canelander	4-270
1966	Countryman 354	6-354			Super 90	GM3.71	Champion 306	6-306	Canelander	4-270
1967	Countryman 354	6-354					Champion 306	6-306	Canelander	4-270
1968	Countryman 354	6-354					Champion 306	6-306	Canelander AP	6-306
1969	Countryman 354	6-354					Champion 306	6-306	Canelander AP	6-306
1970	Countryman C6100	6-354	Champion 236	4-270			Champion C670L	6-306	Canelander AP	6-306
1971	Countryman C6100	6-354	(236B/L/DB)	4-270			Champion C670L	6-306	Canelander AP	6-306
1972	Countryman C6100	6-354	(236B/L/DB)	4-270	C456	4-212	Champion C670L	6-306	Canelander AP	6-306
1973	Countryman C6100	6-354	(236L/DB)	4-270	C456	4-212	Champion C670L	6-306		
1974	Countryman C6100	6-354	(236L)	4-270	C456	4-212	Champion C670L	6-306		Deere
1975	Countryman C6100	6-354	(236L)	4-270			Champion C670L	6-306	Champion 239	4-239

John Deere Engined Models

Year	Model	Engine	Model	Engine	Model	Engine	Model	Engine
1975	3380	4-239	4080	6-329	4280	6-359	4480	6T-359
1976	3380	4-239	4080	6-329	4280	6-359	4480	6T-359
1977	3380	4-239	4080	6-329	4280	6-359	4480	6T-359
1978	3380	4-239	4080	6-329	4280	6-359	4480	6T-359
1979	3380	4-239	4080	6-329	4280	6-359	4480	6T-359
1980	3380	4-239	4080	6-329	4280	6-359	4480	6T-359
1981	3380	4-239	4080	6-329	4280	6-359	4480	6T-359
1982	3380	4-239	4080	6-329	4280	6-359	4480	6T-359
1983	3380	4-239	4080	6-329	4280	6-359	4480	6T-359
1983	3380B	4-239	4080B	6-329	4280B	6-359	4480B	6T-359
1984	3380B	4-239	4080B	6-329	4280B	6-359	4480B	6T-359
1985	3380B	4-239	4080B	6-329	4280B	6-359	4480B	6T-359
1985	4090	6-359	4290	6T-359	4490	6T-466	4690	6T-466
1986	4090	6-359	4290	6T-359	4490	6T-466	4690	6T-466

1987 on....... Waterloo & Mannheim built imported tractors

Notes: First style: 40K, 40KA, 45KA, 55KA, 55D/DA, 60DA, first Super 70s, and Champion 6G.

1958-59 Intermediate Style

Later Super 70s and Super 90

Champion 9G	1959-65
Countryman Mark 1	1958-59
Countryman Mark 2	1960
Countryman Mark 3	1961-62
Countryman 6	1963-65
Canelander	1959-67
Crusader	1959-62

Last Chamberlain Style

Champion 306	1966-70
Countryman 354	1966-70
Canelander "AP"	1968-72
Champion 236 Series	1970-75
Champion C670L	1970-75
Countryman C6100	1970-75
C456	1972-74
Chamberlain-Deere 239	1975-76